MW01481951

Morgan,

May you have a long lasting love life with your husband!

Delenee 2010

Happily Wed & Happily Fed

Recipes for Love

Delenee Brugman

iUniverse, Inc.
New York   Bloomington

Happily Wed and Happily Fed
Recipes for Love

iUniverse books may be ordered through booksellers or by contacting:

iUniverse
1663 Liberty Drive
Bloomington, IN 47403
www.iuniverse.com
1-800-Authors (1-800-288-4677)

ISBN: 978-1-4401-6502-3 (pbk)
ISBN: 978-1-4401-6503-0 (cloth)
ISBN: 978-1-4401-6501-6 (ebk)

Printed in the United States of America

iUniverse rev. date: 9/21/2009

Dedicated to my Glenn.
You are my love.

Garlic, onions, and butter slowly simmering … gets you every time

Acknowledgments

To Glenn:
  Thank you for allowing me to unveil our stories. I love you.

To my friends and family:
  I held your positive messages of encouragement in my heart, and they echoed through me as I wrote.

To Mary:
  Thank you for capturing my moments and reflecting life with me. Photographs by Mary Podgurski: Wedding Day; One of life's greatest gifts … children; Walk toward your future together.

$\mathcal{E}xcerpts$

THE PROPOSAL DINNER

 $\mathcal{M}$ y whole day was reserved in preparation of our evening together …. I decided to create a night he would not forget and plotted to encircle him in my love nest, so that he would never want to leave it.

Delicious thoughts streamed through my head for the plans …. *What should I make him for dinner? Ah, yes, I'll seduce him with my salmon. He'll be mesmerized after he tastes it. How about dessert? Well, I've never made a fresh summer peach pie before, but it can't be that hard. Okay, clean the apartment, shop for ingredients, don't forget candles, and I'll wear my 501 jeans with my boyfriend tee—braless.* He was hungry when he arrived. To my delight, the salmon came out beautifully. It was so delicious that despite my ruining the pie—an inedible disaster of crunchy uncooked peaches in a soupy mess on top of a soggy crust—the next day he proposed!

Baked Salmon, White Wine, and Capers

NEVER SAY THE "D" WORD

 $\mathcal{T}$ rust me on this. I mean it. Regardless of what he did or how mad and hurt you are, you can never, ever say, "I want a divorce." The "D" word is the death of a marriage. Remember that. Your need to say it will pass. Be patient. If you are contemplating divorce, please take the entire afternoon instead to quietly and patiently contemplate how you can heal your marriage, perhaps with the help of my words and my stories, while making my most treasured recipe. It will fill your home with sweet and savory aromas, nourish your body, and soothe your aching, wounded heart.

Baked Apple and Butternut Squash Soup

APPRECIATION

The next morning at Café Reese, a tall, beautiful woman with short, bobbed red hair and green eyes requested to meet me. She came by the café the evening before for a glass of wine and was surprised to see that we were closed. When she heard why, she wanted to meet the woman who could get her husband to close his restaurant (on Mother's Day) to make her fried chicken. She walked right up to me, smiled, looked me in the eye, and shook my hand.

Papa's Fried Chicken

ROLE CHANGES

Marriage is much like a dramatic play. There are many scenes and many acts. You will wear different costumes and change hats during its production. A mutual understanding between you and your husband regarding who plays what role in the marriage and when is fundamental. Remain flexible and be willing to change roles by letting go of gender stigmatism and stereotypes. Choose roles that utilize your personal strengths and allow you to contribute to the team in the best way that makes you happy. When the partners are happy in their roles, the team becomes strong, and the marriage functions well.

… When I've got Baked Potato Cheese Soup pre-baking in the oven, I'll flip open my laptop, power up the Wi-Fi, and scan the latest real estate listings on the Web—hunting for our next investment and crunching numbers in my head as I cook, happily fulfilled in my multiple roles.

Baked Potato Cheese Soup

GRACE AND RESILIENCE

Some years you will experience enormous amounts of stress and great change. Glenn and I are proof that a marriage can survive during tough times: Surprise, we're pregnant! A beloved parent passes. You're fired! (Uh—that one happened to me.) Unemployment. Illness. Relocation. Four and a half years of monthly orthodontic bills for two smiling girls. Refinanced the house—again. What else? The family dog died. Didn't get that promotion we were counting on. Want more? The roof of our fixer-upper home leaked all across the center beam, and we didn't have enough buckets, pots, pans, or towels to mop up the tropical storm pouring in. Our eldest teen ...

Comfort food: Roasted Pepper Marinara

SUPPORT

Before we served Coconut Cream Mahi Mahi over jasmine rice to our guests who traveled across the Pacific Ocean to celebrate with us, Glenn surprised me by standing up and giving me a toast thanking me for my love, patience, and support. He told everyone that he couldn't have earned his MBA without me and then presented me with a ring box holding inside three thin bands carved like bamboo and bonded together.

He said to me, "The copper band represents the past, the gold band represents the present, and the platinum band represents our future together." The guests were teary-eyed and burst into applause. I was touched, and I still am. I wear these rings around my neck on a long, braided gold chain. During those four years of support, you bet I made a lot of meals! I would set plates of food on his desk and leave the room, quietly closing the door behind me.

Coconut Cream Mahi Mahi

Contents

The Recipes

Flirt

COMMUNICATE

LOVE

ENDURE

Introduction

Dear Reader,

May you be fulfilled in love and in life, and enjoy every meal along the way! This delicious love story—my marriage to Glenn—is intertwined with recipes for a happier marriage and recipes for savory meals I've passionately prepared for our family for more than twenty years. My immediate desire for this book is to satiate a hunger I recognize in today's marriages and to enrich the endless pursuit of nourishment. My vision, however, is to inspire longevity in marriages by encouraging you to embrace your marriage as robustly, creatively, and optimistically as I have.

I begin this cookbook for love from our restful home in Kula, Maui, Hawaii, during the twentieth year of our marriage. We have come a long way. Our journey of love, friendship, struggles, joy, and cherished family times are bonded together by great meals. We have survived against many odds: divorce statistics, parental history (multiple marriages and divorces of both my parents), and the *unbelievable* truth that we met, kissed, got pregnant, and married all within four and a half months!

This book resembles a memoir. I have added odd family tidbits and humorous mishaps to keep you entertained. You will come to understand what pulling a "Wilson" means and walk through twenty years of life with me. I have not researched the topic of marriage, nor am I a psychiatrist or psychologist. I have lived it. I am a wife sharing with you what works for my marriage.

I also share with you our treasured family recipes. I have not formally studied culinary arts; I have, probably much like you, learned as I cooked. You will enjoy home-cooked meals originating from around the world, including Mexico, the Philippines, France, Italy, Hawaii, and India. Several of these dishes have also been well loved by customers at Café Reese, the popular Portland café I co-created with Glenn.

Our marriage, like many, has not always thrived. There have been starvation periods. It has had dark storms, disappointments, trials, and moments of exasperation felt by both partners. Our marriage is not perfect, nor should it be. It is alive, changing, and growing, as we live within its unfolding story. At its best, it is a good example of the commitment to the most important long-standing human relationship two adults can share. I hope my marriage tips and recipes will resonate with you. What works for me and for my marriage can work for you, too.

Throughout this book, I portray a traditional role for wives in wonderful ways. That is what usually suits my marriage. But please remember that I am also an entrepreneur, a real estate investor, a restaurant owner, and now a writer. Being a wife today is an interesting balance. I write from a wife's perspective because that is what I know. Men like this book, too. Should you be a husband reading this, just flip the words he/him/husband to she/her/wife and many chapters will apply. My marriage tips work for new marriages; old marriages; first, second, or third marriages; or for people wanting to enhance their love relationships and stay committed. I offer you recipes for feeding your marriage and recipes for feeding your family. You can absorb them all at once and change immediately, practice them once a week, or reread them for inspiration when you need to. That recipe is up to you.

My uncle Fred, who has been married to my aunt Lynn for forty years, encouraged me to finish this book and said, "It might add spice to a marriage that in the beginning had all the right ingredients, but over time needs additional sauce."

There is one more thing you should know: I have actually prepared at least 15,000 meals for Glenn. Do the math! That would be approximately two meals per day times 365 days per year for twenty years. This is one great way to show your partner love.

Delenee

Cooking Notes

Feeding your husband and your family is one of the most loving acts you can do for them. It's also one of the most rewarding.

TASTE THE LOVE

Your loving hands give pleasure and health to those who devour your meals. Have loving thoughts as you cook—they can taste the love. When you sit down to dinner, rejoice in the exquisite feeling of giving.

LOVE THE EARTH

Be mindful of the ingredients you use. How was the food grown—with or without pesticides? In what country was it harvested? How humanely was the animal treated in offering you its milk, its eggs, its life? How was mother earth impacted by your use of that ingredient? What positive business practices does the company who packaged your ingredient adhere to? Your choices affect the world around you through the laws of supply and demand.

BAKE IT OR ROAST IT

Bake it or roast it if you can. The oven starts and finishes many meals for me, allowing a busy wife a little more time. I even pre-bake ingredients for soups. Walk in the door, set down your keys, and preheat your oven.

THE MAGIC WAND

An electric handheld puree wand is an essential tool in my kitchen.

FRUITS AND VEGETABLES

Sneak them in! Add vegetables, greens, or fruits as a side dish to every recipe in this book. Many of the recipes can be put right on top of a hearty salad or served with one. I have two tricks to help you sneak them into your daily diet. (1) Wash your fruits and keep them in a bowl out on the kitchen counter or on the table where they are easily accessible. If they are stored in plastic bags in the crisper of the refrigerator, the old saying holds true: out of sight, out of mind. (2) Purchase pre-washed and/or pre-cut salad greens and vegetables and stock your refrigerator with them. You will eat more of them if it is less work to do so.

PRESENTATION

You will see this word at the end of many recipes. I believe that the presentation of the foods you prepare is an important final step in cooking. Color, texture, balance, height, weight, and pairings and even the dishes, silverware, napkins, table accessories, and lighting are all aesthetically valuable in enticing the appetite and soothing the eye. Be creative in your daily presentations—variety is the spice of life.

VEGETARIAN RECIPES

When you see a (v) next to the recipe name, it offers vegetarian options by either eliminating the meat or replacing it with tempeh or tofu. Or, it is a meatless dish in and of itself. Chicken broth can usually be replaced with vegetable broth.

The Recipes

$\mathscr{F}$LIRT

Make Feel Good

The story of us

Nervously fidgeting in my seat, in a small old theater on Polk Street in San Francisco, I watched the other untrained want-to-be actors—my classmates—get called up on the tiny stage to hash out dramatic performance exercises, which to me made us look like fools. The idea of getting up on that stage and playing out exaggerated roles with worn-out props as the other participants in class had done was daunting. I could only concentrate on my fear of being called next. I am shy and prone to fainting spells and unusual mishaps. I wondered, *what in the world am I doing here? Surely, I will trip going up those rickety wood stairs onto the stage, my skirt will fly up, and I will die of embarrassment before I even get to read one line. Did I actually pay for this, and do I really want to try and be an actress—in San Francisco?* My left leg began to quiver involuntarily. It was a beautiful summer afternoon, and I could easily have walked right out of that basement theater. Then my world pivoted.

A very good-looking, dark-haired young man caught my eye on stage. I remember his T-shirt standing out in my mind. It had four large black block letters printed on it that read: YOGA. Within a minute of gazing at him, I had the most wonderful sensations and feelings. As I peered at him, a mixture of joy, curiosity, and a sense of knowingness descended upon me. I knew he would be significant in my life, but I had no idea just how much. The year was 1987. I was twenty-six, and he was twenty-seven.

"Attention actors!" the instructor bellowed from center stage. "For

1

next week's scene partner presentation, you are to deliver your lines in one of two ways. Either make your scene partner feel good or make them feel bad." We were each to deliver our scripted lines with the unspoken intention to make our scene partner either feel good or feel bad. Before we spoke our lines, we were to analyze each one, deciding how we would deliver it, or say it, to our scene partner. Then we would add the dialect and emotion to back up the intention.

This acting lesson is applicable to real life and was the kick-start of our relationship. Before you speak to your husband, ask yourself this question: Am I saying this to make him feel good or bad? If the latter is true, it might be appropriate to rethink what you're saying or how you're saying it.

The rest of the "story of us," as we call it, evolved rapidly. By the end of the class, Glenn (the yoga T-shirt-wearing want-to-be actor guy) nonchalantly leaned back in his chair and from across five rows of theater seats looked right at me and asked me to be his next scene partner. Apparently I had caught his eye, too. It's a good thing because there was a real creep sitting next to me who was pining for my telephone number in hopes of getting together three times (the required amount) as scene partners before the next class.

"My name is Glenn," he said, smiling. I melted. We agreed to meet the following week at the mini-mansion he was living at in the Marina district. We were rehearsing a scene from *9½ Weeks* (just kidding … that's how Glenn likes to tell the story). We were really rehearsing a short scene from the play *The Rainmaker*. The scene was between the two main characters. It was a scene leading up to a kiss.

We rehearsed the scene over and over and over again, flirting with each other and acting out our characters' intentions. Make feel good. Make feel bad. Make feel good. Make feel bad. By the third scene-partner date, we couldn't wait to see each other.

We met at my studio apartment across town on Page Street. I wore a white T-shirt and jeans. Funny thing is, so did Glenn. I suggested we go up on my building's rooftop to rehearse. I had whipped up cool, refreshing berry smoothies, which we carried up the narrow roof access stairs. We now lovingly refer to that afternoon as "berry bliss." It was, after all, a very hot summer day. On the rooftop, in the sun, in our white T-shirts and jeans, in the summer of 1987, with berries on our lips, we went on to the next page of the script and kissed … and we have never stopped. There wasn't much scene rehearsing after our first kiss on that day. We talked and kissed for hours lying on the rooftop until he had to go teach yoga at 4:30 PM.

Berry Bliss (v)

To your health

This recipe seems too simple to be this good and this good for you, but I wouldn't change a thing. It's deliciously nutritious.

Prep time: 5 minutes
Serves: 2 (1 cup each)

½ cup frozen mixed berries (no sugar added blackberries, blueberries, and raspberries)
½ cup frozen bananas (freeze in peeled slices inside freezer bags ahead of time)
100 percent pure apple juice (about 1½ cups)

In a blender add mixed berries and bananas. Pour apple juice until the fruit floats and blend until smooth. Add more apple juice, if needed, to create desired consistency. It will blend into a gorgeous color of deep berry red.

PRESENTATION
Go ahead—add a cocktail umbrella.

$\mathcal{F}$ive Seconds of "Eye Love You"

The proposal dinner

$\mathcal{A}$man held in reverence by his wife is a king. What if after twenty years you could look across the room at your husband with such passion and love for him and for whom you are together that you beam with pride, joy, and thankfulness inside and out? You actually glow with the glory of your love, and he can see it. What would that feel like to you? Do you want that? If the answer is yes, then create that feeling *today*, so you can experience it tomorrow and twenty years from now.

The enticing and flirtatious look of love beamed toward your man says it all. It says, "I love you, I know you. I am here for you. I desire you. I am proud of you. I support you. I am your friend. We share a secret. You are the most important man on earth."

How long does it take to convey this kind and loving message? Five seconds of eye contact—or five second of eye love you. Meet his eyes, radiate your love from deep within yourself, and with a slight smile, beam it in his direction. Your husband will feel everything that you beam toward him and will do anything to bask in the exquisite reception of the rays of love you shine for him.

He will not only feel like the luckiest man alive but will undoubtedly also send this message right back to you. I can only describe it as nurturing waves of warmth and joy resonating in my soul. I can feel this back from Glenn in five seconds, and I gave him "the look of love" just before I served him this dinner.

My whole day was reserved in preparation for our evening together. My new boyfriend, Glenn, whom I was madly in love with, was coming over to my studio apartment for a home-cooked meal—a real bachelor magnet—and I wanted it to be perfect. I decided to create a night he would not forget and plotted to encircle him in my love nest, so that he would never want to leave it.

Delicious thoughts streamed through my head for the plans … *What should I make him for dinner? Ah, yes, I'll seduce him with my salmon. He'll be mesmerized after he tastes it. How about dessert? Well, I've never made a fresh summer peach pie before, but it can't be that hard. Okay, clean the apartment, shop for ingredients, don't forget candles, and … I'll wear my 501 jeans with my boyfriend tee—braless.*

He was hungry when he arrived. To my delight, the salmon came out beautifully. It was so delicious that despite my ruining the pie—an inedible disaster of crunchy uncooked peaches in a soupy mess on top of a soggy crust—the next day he proposed!

Wedding Day

Baked Salmon, White Wine, and Capers

Prep time: 10 minutes
Cook time: 20 minutes
Serves: 2

2 4-ounce salmon steaks or fillets
A small bunch of fresh dill, chopped
¼ cup butter
The juice of half a lemon
1 tablespoon of capers
½ cup of Chardonnay wine
Sea salt
Freshly ground pepper

Preheat your oven to 350°F.
Warm all of the ingredients (except the salmon) for 30 seconds in the microwave to liquefy the sauce. Pour a little of the sauce on the bottom of a baking dish (about ¼ cup) and coat the bottom of the dish so the salmon does not stick. Place the salmon in the dish and then pour the sauce all over the salmon. Bake covered for 15 minutes and then remove the lid for the last 5 minutes to brown the top.

PRESENTATION
A glass of chardonnay to complement the wine in the salmon is a perfect union.

Belly Dancing

The sexiest night of his life just got better

Encircling Glenn in my love nest continues, twenty years later. May 30, 2007, was the sexiest night of my husband's life. I know. I planned it. In my personal story below, I will share with you part of the evening's allure.

Find your evening allure with your husband. What fascinates him? What are his fantasies? What is thrilling to him? What scares him? What does he secretly desire but cannot ask you to do? What does he want? What makes him desire you? What makes his heart skip? Do you know your husband? Do you wish for him to have the best night of his life? Best nights turn into more good nights and then good days and then good weeks, months, and years. We must inspire ourselves to create cherished memories. Fill your life with them. These are the memories we live for. What else is there?

Turning age forty-five was humbling. I realized the good genes I inherited were fading and that if I was lucky enough to walk this earth another forty-five years then I had better start exercising. I've always disliked sports and, well, frankly, exercise too.

That year, on a whim, I purchased a belly dancing DVD and became instantly hooked. I found the movement natural and rhythmic. Before I knew it, twenty minutes were up! To keep me moving, I made it a goal to give Glenn a belly dance performance for his birthday. I practiced three times a week for three months when he was not home. My body began to change. I began to change. I felt great.

At sunset on his birthday in the loft, I lit the room full of candles;

put on the DVD (music only); poured him a glass of dark, rich Merlot; and placed a cigar, lighter, and ashtray on the table next to his favorite armchair. Nervous, excited, and barefoot, wearing a traditional belly-dancing outfit (gold coins and all) in his favorite color, burgundy, I posed in the center of the room. Then I called him upstairs. Ladies, if you could have seen the look on my husband's face, you would do *anything* to re-create it. Gentlemen, what wouldn't you give to be able to smoke a cigar in the house while your wife performs a sexy birthday dance for you?

My heart raced and skipped. I couldn't believe that I would feel timid and apprehensive in front of my husband of twenty years! I was rekindling the lusty, flirty feelings we had when we first met, and I felt young and exhilarated. My dance certainly entertained him. I performed it well.

Wanting to remain in the alluring exotic atmosphere, for his birthday dinner I cooked him his favorite dish—Indian Curried Chicken. The sexiest night of his life just got better. We dined alfresco on our deck, lit with hurricane lamps amidst the warm humid Maui evening air. We filled our terracotta bowls with jasmine rice and topped it with the deep savory spices of the curried chicken and sweet ginger chutney. Glenn is very quiet when he eats his favorite dish and likes to take his time. It was a lovely evening.

Indian Curried Chicken

Prep time: 20 minutes
Cook time: 30 minutes
Serves: 4 to 6

MAIN DISH

1 pound boneless, skinless chicken sliced into bite-sized strips
3 tablespoons butter
1½ tablespoons yellow curry powder
2 tablespoons white wine
1 tablespoon fresh squeezed lemon juice
1 cup carrots cut into ¼-inch rounds
1 cup partially peeled and cubed russet potatoes
1 cup cubed yellow onion
1 cup each cubed green, red, and yellow bell peppers
1 tablespoon crushed garlic
1½ cups chicken broth
1½ cups heavy cream
Salt
Freshly ground black pepper
2 cups jasmine rice

GARNISHES

(Very important to complete the dish):
A handful of chopped, fresh cilantro
A handful of cashews
A handful of raisins
1 tablespoon per serving of store-bought ginger-mango chutney

Follow package directions to make the jasmine rice. Salt and pepper the chicken and brown it in a deep skillet with the butter and curry, covered for 10 minutes on medium/low heat. Add all other ingredients (except the cream) and simmer on medium/low heat, covered for 20 minutes. Warm the cream and stir it in at the end.

PRESENTATION

Serve Indian Curried Chicken in deep bowls over jasmine rice and garnish with the cilantro, cashews, raisins, and chutney. I serve it with a fresh green salad and make a vinaigrette using the chutney: Whisk together 3 tablespoons of olive oil with 1 tablespoon of balsamic vinegar and 2 tablespoons of chutney.

Change the Routine
Hotel lust

Do "it" in other places. That's all I'm going to say! How can I write more? I know my kids will read this and my parents and Glenn's mom and probably the neighbors, so you'll have to trust me on this. Play out your fantasies and enjoy each other in a new environment. It is liberating to occasionally be freed of the routine and the humdrum of the marital bed.

I'd like to thank the wonderful hospitality and cherished privacy of the W Hotels in NYC and Honolulu, the Waikiki Outrigger, The Sheraton Maui, The Hyatt Waikiki, The Grand Wailea, The Kaanapali Hyatt, The Fairmont Kea Lani, The Westin Maui Resort & Spa, The Raddison Kauai, The Hilton Waikaloa, The Hotel Lanai, The Manele Bay Hotel, Spannochia Villa & Organic Farm, Tuscany, Italy, The Bolivar Hotel, Rome, The Hotel Paris, The Bellafonte, The San Diego Surfer Inn, The Oregon Coast Shamrock Lodgettes, The Best Western Hood River, and many more B&Bs in the Pacific Northwest.

Room Service for Two

A recipe for indulgence

$\mathcal{N}$ow that you've taken me up on the marriage tip, "Change the Routine," don't leave the hotel room for hours. Pick up that big black menu by the phone and dial room service. It's expensive but so worth it. Get whatever you want. How often will you really get the chance to do this? Take it while you can.

So many times at restaurants or in hotels we think to ourselves, *oh that's too expensive,* or *we should share it,* or *I really shouldn't,* etc. But, a lovely dose of decadence goes a long, long way for your soul and for your marriage. It's okay to indulge.

I speak from experience. Unexpectedly, at our hotel, late at night and well past the dinner hour, Glenn and I each ordered tureens of French onion soup, big New York steaks with fat baked potatoes and all the trimmings, salads, and a bottle of Merlot. Our hotel waiter, wearing a black suit, rolled in a cart adorned with crisp white linens and dinner plates covered with fancy silver lids. I remember appreciating the simple flowers resting in a clear glass on the table as the waiter opened our wine. For dessert we shared a banana split. We merrily ate and drank for well over an hour on the bed, happy and naked underneath our fluffy white cotton hotel robes, smiling and enjoying each other and the food.

There were no distractions; there was nothing to "do," nothing to clean, and nothing to worry about. I think that hotel dinner, with tip, cost us two hundred dollars, but it was some of the best money we ever spent on a meal and on us. That hotel room service treated our marriage to pure luxury. It is one of the most relaxing times we have enjoyed together, and the memory of this night is a long lasting one.

The "Wow" Factor

Men are visual creatures

Ladies, what have you been wearing lately? Are you in baby drool T-shirts and elastic waistband denim jeans that really do make your butt look big? Or are you in "don't mess with me" business suits? Either way, it may be time for a change.

Men are visual creatures. When was the last time you wore a low-cut dress and put on some lip-gloss? Ask yourself this question: Would my husband be turned on or turned off if he did my laundry today? Most men would like to see and think about you as you were when you first met. If he proposed to an athletic blonde with short cropped hair and a zest for life, make sure that girl still exists, somewhat, in the best way she can, even twenty years later.

Do I need to mention diet and exercise? You know what you need to do there. A perfect body does not exist, but you do want to look attractive, sexy, and approachable to your husband. So, maybe this girl he proposed to is twenty pounds heavier. He probably doesn't care as much as you do. Men prefer soft, round flesh. It's true! Don't worry about it. Emphasize your assets. You want him to appreciate the whole package.

Put on a pair of sexy shoes once in a while. High heels make the leg look elongated and emphasize the calf muscles, plus it's a good way to show off your ankle tattoo if you've got one. I personally can't wear heels for more than a couple of hours. I never really figured out how to walk in them! The last time I wore heels a woman at my hair salon said I looked like a child playing dress up in my mother's shoes, wobbling around. But, I do wear them out to dinner with my husband, to spice up my wow factor. Just sit down, cross your legs, and give him a smile. He will appreciate the effort. That's it in a nutshell—make an effort.

Is it time for a makeover? Change with the times. Get updated. Go to the cosmetics counter and ask them for natural makeup tips to camouflage imperfections and tricks to highlight your good features. Makeup worn properly can create an amazing transformation. What about the hair? Change hairdressers. Get a manicure and a pedicure. Spend a few hundred dollars on yourself (yes, you can) once a year to keep yourself in the now and in the "wow" of your husband's eyes.

One Saturday morning I motivated (okay, I begged) the family to do some yard work. When they agreed, in haste, I just grabbed some clothes out of my dresser, got dressed, brushed my teeth, and ran outside to delegate. Thinking only about those darn weeds in the flowerbeds that the kids could pull and the tree trimming Glenn could do, I wasn't concerned with how I appeared.

When I came indoors a few hours later to thank them by preparing lunch, I caught a glimpse of myself in the mirror. "Good grief," I said out loud, aghast. The image that appeared back to me in the mirror said, frump. I was wearing stained, baggy, cut off, knee-length jean shorts; a straw "granny" hat; no makeup, glasses; an old, oversized man's T-shirt (Glenn's); and my scruffy tennis shoes with gray knee-high socks that were bunched down.

I immediately marched upstairs and gave myself a gardening make over. I traded my glasses for my contact lenses and put on a little makeup (a hit of mascara and some lip gloss), cute shorts, a better T-shirt, my nice tennis shoes with ankle socks, and a straw cowboy hat. Daisy Duke was not staring back at me in the mirror, but it was an enormous improvement.

With a platter of our favorite panini in hand—turkey, ginger-mango chutney, and provolone—I called them from the deck, "Time for lunch!" My youngest looked up at me first and said, "Hey Mom, you look cute." And my husband put down his shears, wiped the sweat from his brow, and with a twinkle in his eye he smiled and said, "Wow."

Turkey Ginger Mango Chutney Panini

"Time for lunch!"
Recipe created by Devin Brugman

Prep time: 5 minutes
Cook time: 5 minutes
Serves: Makes 4 sandwiches

8 slices of your favorite bread
½ cup olive oil
½ cup mayonnaise
12 slices roasted turkey
1 cup store-bought ginger-mango chutney
4 slices provolone cheese

For the best results, use a panini grill. A toaster oven works, too. Lightly baste the outside of the bread with olive oil. Thinly coat the inside of the bread with mayonnaise. Lay 3 turkey slices out and spoon a tablespoon of ginger-mango chutney down the center. Fold in half. Line up all 3 folded slices of turkey on 1 side of bread and top with a slice of provolone cheese and the other slice of bread.

Grill in the panini grill 5 minutes until the provolone is melted, and the sandwich is golden brown. The chutney becomes warm and oozes out in sweet, tangy bites.

PRESENTATION

Our favorite way to eat this is with baked pita chips and fresh carrot sticks, which we dip in roasted red pepper humus. In the fall, replace the ginger-mango chutney with cranberry-apple chutney.

ate

Time spent together enriches unity

When was the last time you two danced? When was the first time? What is your song? Go buy it and play it in the car on the way to out to dinner. You are going on a date with your husband, the most attractive man alive, because he's yours. It is likely that you will be the one who has to initiate the date and make all the arrangements. Do it without resentment and create an atmosphere conducive to talking.

Who wants to get married and never go on a date again? Has it been so long since you've had a quiet moment alone that you've forgotten what brought the two of you together? Do you remember that first spark? Reminisce about the first time you saw each other. Describe the chemistry. Laugh about it. Enjoy the "us." Talk about the original dreams you had when you first decided to share your lives. Have you achieved them? Can you still? Do you need to create new dreams? Acknowledge how far you've come—together.

Toward the end of the date, decide on a weekly date night and ask your husband to plan the next one. Leave the details up to his discretion. Tell him that the next date need not be so serious. Once you reconnect your love spark, are communicating well, and are moving forward in your lives together, the next date should be fun. Don't try and control it. As the time nears, mention to him how much you are looking forward to your upcoming date.

Recently, I spontaneously took Glenn to pizza in the Portland Pearl District to break up the humdrum of the nightly question, "What should we make for dinner?" The evening wasn't spectacular, but it was nice. We sat outside on a picnic bench with our little dog and enjoyed the warm summer air. We didn't speak of anything important or memorable and went home to go to bed early. I didn't think much of it. The next morning (in public) Glenn came up to me and gave me a big hug, a kiss and said, "Thanks for our date last night, honey." His pleased reaction came as a surprise to me. I thought, *how could an hour of pizza with me make him so happy?* Then, I realized that even a simple evening out honors marriage. Time spent together enriches unity.

Here's a list of twenty-five date ideas for you and your hubby, followed by the recipe for date night number eight.

1. Sunset picnic (bring curried chicken salad, luscious lemon squares, and a bottle of Pinot Gris)

2. Star gazing (summer's eve on the lawn; bring blankets, pillows, binoculars, cherries, chocolates, and Pinot Noir)

3. Night club (jazz, disco, rock … be sure to dance!)

4. Rock concert (act like you're seventeen again)

5. Dance lessons (salsa is sexy, tango is sexier)

6. Horse races (bet your wedding date numbers)

7. Drag races (pick a favorite car together)

8. Strip poker & charcuterie (late evening—master bedroom)

9. Dinner theater (fun and entertaining)

10. Dinner out with another married couple (imperative)

11. Matinee (sneak away midweek, midday)

12. Sunday morning café enjoying espresso and croissants; no need to chat … just be together reading the paper

13. Test drive a sports car (or rent one for the day)

14. Train ride, boat ride, hayride, helicopter ride, horseback ride, etc.

15. Cooking class

16. Massage (check local listings for massage schools; half the price and just as nice)

17. Walk in a forest

18. Yoga class, pilates class, the gym

19. Charity (volunteer together at a soup kitchen, church, school, or animal shelter)

20. Lecture/seminar (dinner or coffee afterwards for some intellectual discussion)

21. Film festival, art festival, etc.

22. Art gallery, car show, museum, or computer show

23. Sports events (take one for the team)

24. Two cocktails in the most expensive hotel in town (have him wear a button-down shirt and cologne for you)

25. Pedicures (yes, men like them, too)

Charcuterie

*Spend time getting yourself preheated. There is
no cooking involved in this recipe.*

Charcuterie is simply a French culinary art of cooked and cured meats. Saying the word "charcuterie" is more intimidating than the food itself. When charcuterie is joined with elegant pairings of cheese and wine, you have a meal that has been satiating man's appetite for centuries.

Learning about cheeses, wines, and cured meats is fun to do and will enhance the evening's allure. Meet your hubby at a gourmet market for lunch to sample delights. Ask a knowledgeable delicatessen a lot of questions. Buy what sounds good to you and take a few risks, too. Choosing charcuterie together during the day is an aphrodisiac to the evening. This gives both of you something to look forward to. Foreplay begins well before you enter the bedroom. Here are some of our favorites for a picnic in bed.

MEATS
Wine-cured salami, thinly sliced prosciutto, double-smoked sausage

CHEESE
Huntsman, Manchego, Gruyère, peppered Brie, Humboldt Fog, Smoked Gouda, Gorgonzola, Vella Dry Jack, Goats milk cheese of any kind (chèvre).

BREADS
French baguettes, crisp crackers, melba toast, crostini

FRUITS
Grapes, tart apples, dried fig or date cakes

NUTS

Roasted and salted hazelnuts, pistachios

OLIVES

Kalamata, Italian mixed olives

WINES

Merlots, red blends, Cabernets, Old Vine Zinfandel

PRESENTATION

I like to offer our newfound treats on a wooden cutting board accessorized with unusual knives, mustards, and chunks of crusty bread that we dip into a dish of three parts olive oil to one part balsamic vinegar, a pinch of sea salt, and a few leaves of fresh rosemary. We eat on the bed, with our hands and with abandon.

COMMUNICATE

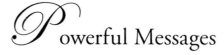

$\mathcal{P}$owerful Messages

Intonation, word choices, and listening.

INTONATION

$\mathcal{E}$xpressing love with your words and with your voice is imperative to keeping your marriage gliding along smoothly, especially through today's exceedingly fast-paced advanced communication systems. Your intonation is key.

We are all so busy responding to e-mails, voicemails, and text messages that they end up burdening our lives just as much as they enhance them. We spend exorbitant amounts of time communicating through these systems. My point here is to create a communication pattern with your husband through this technological maze that he can count on as a positive.

Communication through technology tends to be impersonal and impatient. Call waiting and instant messaging are interruptions creating urgency in an already stressful world. Be the sweet voice at the other end of the line. Your relationship with your husband can be a quiet retreat within your hearts and your voice a reminder of it. Lead him back to you. Soften your voice. Soften your sentences. Ask yourself, "Will this conversation, e-mail, voicemail, or text message make him want to hug me tonight?" When caller ID shows up with your name on it or he sees an e-mail from you, he should be happy to receive it.

I admit to sometimes being guilty of manipulating my husband and our conversations by complaining, ordering, arguing, raising my voice, using the silent treatment, sighing, impatience, whining, and shortness. This is the area of improvement I need to work on most as a wife. I work daily on my patience, kindness, and the intonation of my voice. It is a practice.

ETERNITY WORDS

"*Happy* ever after" and "forever" are wonderful eternity words. Speak them to each other as often as possible. The ones I recommend that you *not* say, especially during an argument, are always and never. Let me give you some examples.

> "You *always* leave the towel on the floor," said the wife.
> "You *never* remember our anniversary," said the wife.
> "You *always* forget to lock the side door," said the husband.
> "You *never* listen to me," said the husband.

Someone does not "always" do something wrong. It would sound better to say, "When I found the towel you left on the floor this morning, I felt frustrated. Could you please remember to hang it up to dry?" When he hangs the towel up to dry, be sure to acknowledge it and thank him. This is very important if you want the positive behavior repeated.

I remember going to a marriage counselor a couple of times the first year we were married. During the first ten minutes of our initial counseling session, we learned about eternity words. We were completely unaware that we spoke in absolutes to each other, but the counselor picked up on it immediately. It is amazing how simply changing a few words can change a situation for the better. We are grateful to have learned this early on.

"The first year of our marriage was the hardest," says Glenn. I don't remember the first year being as hard as he does. Maybe he just couldn't say how challenging it was for him then, until now.

NEVER SAY THE "D" WORD

Trust me on this. I mean it. Regardless of what he did or how mad and hurt you are, you can never, ever say, "I want a divorce."

The "D" word is the death of a marriage. Remember that. Your need to say it will pass. Be patient. Emotions are like currents; they ebb and flow. Difficult situations will evolve, and resolutions will come forth. Trust that they will, in time. Just don't say the "D" word, ever.

I know a couple that loosely tosses the phrase out when talking about each other, and they threaten each other with divorce every time they argue. Don't throw this hurtful phrase in your spouse's face in the heat of the moment or in a negative mood. You can't erase that "D" once you've said it. Once said, it is difficult to remove its weight. Respect your spouse and yourself. Respect the marriage! You made a commitment for happy ever after—why then would you ever dishonor yourself, your word, your promise, and your marriage? Get working positively toward solutions to your problems, instead of poisoning your marriage with the big, ugly "D."

Glenn and I promised early in our marriage to never say the "D" word. Coming from a background of multiple divorces in my family, I knew we had to be firm about this rule. Each of us has, a few times, started to or wanted to say the other no-no words—"leave" or "separate"—but the feeling and moment passed. It does. Once, I literally bit my tongue to keep from speaking, and I could only communicate through nodding. It worked.

ALWAYS SAY THE "WE" WORD

When you are talking with your spouse, to your friends, to your family, and especially to yourself, always reference your life in terms of "we" instead of "me."

The ego is large. It has been fed a diet of independence, self-sufficiency, and self-centeredness by society. Try to keep it in check. The ego can bulldoze a marriage right into the ground.

I had an epiphany when Glenn mentioned to me that many times when I spoke to him I would reference "me," instead of "we." It had not occurred to me that I was doing this. Once I became aware of the "we" word and began to use it, I could see that Glenn really responded positively. Every time I said "we," I reinforced our relationship. I think the "me" word sounded like nails on a chalkboard to him. It became a verbal distraction to the point that all he could hear was "me, me, me," and he could not actually focus on the subject I was talking about.

Once I got into the habit of saying "we" (it did not come naturally due to my inflated ego), our relationship strengthened. "We" became "us," and this idea gave me great security. I like saying it now. It has importance. Again, some of the smallest gestures can have a big impact.

Listening

*S*ometimes Glenn and I talk over each other. Sometimes we shout, "You're not listening!" Sometimes we think we know exactly what the other will say, so we don't let the other finish their sentence, and we discredit the other by doing so. Then we shout, "Let me finish!"

The longer you are married, the harder you will have to listen. You haven't heard it all, even after twenty years. You cannot predict what the other will say or how he will interpret an event. The longer you are together, the more important it becomes to stay present in a conversation by giving your undivided attention to your spouse. Everyone wants to be heard and understood. We have a fundamental need for recognition and validation. We project outwardly, trying to communicate, "This is who I am; this is how I understand the situation; this is how I think; this is how I interpret the world and me in it."

Let him finish his sentence. Don't interrupt. Have empathy. Your point can be made later. Do you always have to be right? Your righteousness could cost you your marriage. I have listened to couples argue their own points relentlessly, and the funny thing is, they were both right.

Really concentrate and listen to what he is saying. Then, before you answer, respond to what he has said, acknowledging his viewpoint. (You don't have to agree, just acknowledge.) Repeat in your own words what he has just said, so he knows that you understand him. Then, when he is finished and there is the appropriate pause in the conversation where he wants your input, give it. Carefully choose your words, particularly if you do not agree with him or are unhappy or worried about his situation. Think before you speak. When you validate your partner's point of view by listening patiently, repeating what you have heard, and responding in a manner conducive to your husband's psyche, he will begin to do the same for you. He will come forward revealing more of himself, safe in your loving, empathetic arms.

A few years ago Glenn had tremendous stress at work. A corporate merger threatened his "secure" management position that he'd given ten years of his life to achieve, and he was worried. A team of mainland executives flew to the islands of Hawaii and took away jobs from the local people who had built the business.

His co-workers were laid off rapidly. There was pressure on Glenn to fire some of his subordinates, whom the executives thought were overpaid, and one awful afternoon I overheard Glenn on the phone in his home office justifying his own position for more than an hour. It was humiliating. The executives cut costs and labor hours, so his territory suffered, and yet they wanted an increase in sales. Although unsurpassed, record-breaking, multimillion-dollar years were a part of Glenn's success for that company, they wanted more, and they rattled the cage he worked in. At that time, I had to be very careful about how I reacted. We had a lot to lose—the company car, three weeks paid vacation, a good salary, and the medical benefits for the family.

Did he anticipate coming to me for loving words of kindness when he hung up the phone? Or would he head out for a cocktail to ease the anxiety? Would he share his fears with me when he got home? The answers to these questions were within me, his wife. It had nothing to do with him. When I carefully conveyed that I would listen to him without judgment, without compounding the situation with my fears, and instead give my unconditional support, his needs were met. He confided in me. He trusted me. We became closer and stronger as a team.

His thinking then becomes positive. *I can handle this. I have a great wife. It's just a job. A job is not my life. My wife is my life. I'm lucky to have her. She really listens and understands me. I think I will cook for her tonight, and that will help me take my mind off these problems.* While he was frying Papa's Tacos and I was chopping the onions, I began to persuade him with subtle suggestions on how he could leave that cage and work for himself, and that we would be fine without that job.

Papa's Tacos

A good recipe "We" make together

There are many variations to making tacos, but this chicken taco recipe is our all-time favorite. We crave these crunchy tacos! The secret is in the frying. Papa (Glenn's father) made hundreds of tacos for dozens of teenagers in southern California in the 1970s. Glenn's brother Monty holds the family record for the most tacos eaten at one time. He ate thirteen.

Prep time: 10 minutes
Cook time: 15 minutes
Serves: Makes 12 tacos

One dozen corn tortillas
2 cups cooked skinless chicken, shredded
2 cups grated good quality mild cheddar cheese
1 small yellow onion, chopped
2 cups shredded green-leaf lettuce
2 large tomatoes, chopped
1 handful of cilantro, chopped (if desired)
Salt
4 cups corn oil for frying

Grate the cheddar cheese. Chop onion, lettuce, tomato, and cilantro. Set aside.

Preheat the corn oil (about ¼-inch deep) in the frying pan. Take $1/3$ cup of the shredded chicken, put it in a single corn tortilla, and grab it with a pair of tongs, folding it into a taco shape. Fry the corn tortilla with the cooked chicken inside until the tortilla is golden brown. Fry 4 tacos simultaneously. Drain on paper towels. The chicken will be crunchy on the ends and very, very tasty. Add the cheese to the taco while it is still warm so it will melt. Salt just before serving.

PRESENTATION

Put the chopped onion, lettuce, tomato, and cilantro in bowls on the table so you can pass the bowls and dress your own tacos. Sour cream, guacamole, salsas, and hot sauces are favorite condiments you may want to add. Pile tacos on a large platter and set in the center of the table. They will disappear.

Dark Moods in Marriage

Don't do damage in the dark

When irritations and annoyances arise in your marriage, be cautious of how you react, even if you think that you can't tolerate them, or him, any longer. Your reaction can be intensified by a low mood. And we all know how moody we can get. However, what you actually need to do to change the situation comes from within you, not from fixing or leaving your spouse. You will need to change your own thoughts and how you inwardly talk to yourself about the issues and about him. This is especially important during a dark mood. If you want a better marriage, work on yourself. Focus on becoming a tolerant and more patient wife and be very, very careful what you say to yourself and to him when in a dark mood. Don't do damage in the dark!

One evening I was in a particularly dark mood. I was negative and complaining to myself about all of the things that irritate me about Glenn. You know, the ones that I think he must change. The things he must do to be the way I think he should be. I was angry because I had told him about these irritating traits over and over again, and he hadn't changed, which to a woman means he's not listening. This behavior by far is my most unbecoming. (The word "nag" comes to mind here.)

I had the good sense to bite my negative tongue and shut my angry self up and headed to the guest room alone. I flipped on the tube and started channel surfing. A TV evangelist came on, and I found myself absolutely captivated by what he said. He was giving a sermon on—what else—marriage. I usually don't watch TV evangelists, by the way, but I do recognize when I am supposed to receive a message. Ironically, this message came at the very moment I was least expecting it, but when I really needed it.

The minister said that we should stop thinking about all of the things that bother us about our partners over and over again (like a broken record repeating itself in our minds). We should stop saying to ourselves, *oh this really bugs me, and I can't stand it anymore,* because compounded negative thoughts like these will result in a level of exasperation that could ultimately end the marriage.

I don't remember the minister's name, his denomination, or the channel I was tuned to; but he suggested a new way of talking to yourself that went something along these lines: *This is my chosen spouse, whom I love and who God sent to me. I honor this man (woman) and our marriage. This is my husband (wife) who has this problem that we can work on together.* This message resonated with me, changed the way I think, and remains with me in my everyday approach to a happier marriage.

If you repeat a positive statement like this to yourself, your mind relaxes, and you naturally start seeking solutions to the problem. You actually feel better and remember what is important, which is to respect the marriage and the man. The bothersome problem is minimized in this perspective. The problem either becomes more acceptable, or you become more accepting, or both. Once this positive attitude is implemented, a more supportive, loving wife and a better relationship ultimately results.

I emerged from the guest room, ready to make dinner. I wasn't saying much as my lesson slowly simmered on the back burner of my mind. A loving meditation poured through me as I made Glenn an earthy, gutsy stew in a rich, deep broth to ease the tension I had created.

Savory Chuck Roast Stew

Prep time: 20 minutes
Cook time: 2 hours
Serves: 6

STEW
2 pounds chuck roast cut into bite-sized cubes
2 tablespoons extra virgin olive oil
2 yellow onions chopped into bite-sized pieces
5 carrots peeled and chopped into 1-inch rounds
1 large ripe beefsteak tomato, quartered
2 cloves garlic, finely chopped
2 tablespoons fresh thyme leaves
2 bay leaves
1 cup Cabernet red wine
5 cups beef stock
6 ounces pancetta (thinly sliced Italian cured ham)

HERBED NOODLES
2 cups wide flat egg noodles
1 tablespoon butter
1 tablespoon Italian parsley, chopped

Salt and pepper the chuck roast cubes and brown them for about 7 minutes in the olive oil with the onions and carrots in a large pot. Add the tomato, garlic, thyme, and bay leaves and sauté 1 more minute. Add the wine, beef stock, and pancetta. Simmer the stew on very low heat until the beef is very tender, covered for about 2 hours.

Meanwhile, boil the egg noodles in a large pot of salted water. Drain and toss them with the butter and Italian parsley.

PRESENTATION
Ladle the stew over a bowlful of the herbed noodles and enjoy it with the rest of the Cabernet wine.

$\mathscr{H}$ow to Fight
Guidelines for communication

THE BOILING POINT

$\mathscr{T}$ry to recognize a build up of simmering issues and address them before you boil over. It is challenging to do, but so helpful in getting your needs met and problems resolved. Women can tolerate a lot, but we tend to hold things inside. Men don't know when we are on the verge of boiling over. Often a fight erupts when your spouse does one little thing that brings you to a boil. It is not the little thing that bothers you, but he doesn't know this. "Why are you so upset that I put the olive oil back in the wrong place?" he will ask, thinking you are neurotic. The olive oil becomes the catalyst for eruption. Stewing is not healthy for your relationship.

DIGNITY

$\mathscr{E}$xercising dignity and respect for your home will help keep safe boundaries during heated conversations or arguments. Please don't fight at a dining table, in your bedroom, the children's bedrooms, or your bathroom. These areas are sacred havens for restoration, nurturing, rest, and peace. Keep them that way.

PUBLICITY

*P*lease don't share your dilemmas with the rest of the world. Arguing in places such as restaurants, shopping malls, grocery stores, and banks is not only rude to others, but also embarrassing for you. Be a lady. Be discrete. Arguing in public adds shame to your fight, which fuels it. Take your problems to a quiet, private place and hash them out in that safe environment where you are both free to communicate without distractions, interruptions, or other people such as children, neighbors, and strangers. Your feelings can wait, even though you think they can't. Say to your spouse, "I am feeling angry, frustrated, hurt (whatever), and I need to talk about it. Where can we talk privately?"

DIVULGING

*D*iscussing your marital problems with the neighbors, his or your colleagues, or his or your parents is risky. Your marital problems are really none of their business, and you may regret divulging personal details later. One true, close, trusted friend (someone who could see your dirty laundry and not judge you) or a professional counselor is a better choice for personal help.

DREDGING

*S*tick to one (or two) problems at a time. Many arguments start out at the boiling point and continue onward to one heated issue after another, with no resolutions in sight, and turn into a full-blown fight. Don't dredge up the past by bringing up other problems and hash them out incessantly every time you argue. Stay focused on the issue at hand and work on solving it.

CHILDREN

*T*here are no good reasons for kids to know about many adult issues. Be a mature and responsible parent. You can never take back negative experiences you create for your children. Even if it is not your intention to damage them emotionally, children are easily bruised. Keep adult issues adult, and private. Exercise self-control. Be careful. Be wise. And wear kid gloves when talking with them about mom and dad. Children, including teenagers, do not have the wherewithal or the emotional maturity to understand adult problems.

One evening, about five years ago, after we had an argument, Glenn took our youngest teen out to dinner. Upon his return, I asked if he told her we were fighting. He paused for a moment and then said, "There is no reason for the kids to know." A grateful tear escaped my left eye. This wise and considerate approach to interpersonal relations is one of the many attributes that I love in Glenn.

I've witnessed other parents trying to get the children on "their side" during a fight, adding ammunition and dysfunction to an already heated arena. This is most unhealthy. If you are in a pattern of this behavior, please seek professional counseling.

I remembered our girls commenting once that they had never seen us fight. I thought to myself, *you must be kidding*! They said that they've heard us argue or talking loudly but had never heard or seen a knockdown, drag out fight. I then thought to myself, *well, we've done something right.*

Children don't need to know about our adult issues. If they are younger than twenty years of age, they probably won't understand. All children want their mom and dad happy, and together. This is not to say that you "fake it" or lie to your children. Just be discrete. The children do not need to be involved. It is your job to protect them, even from yourself at times. This shows respect for your family. But don't close them off altogether either. You don't want them imagining something worse than it is or feeling excluded. It is a delicate balance. Try to teach them relationship skills—empathy, patience, and endurance—by setting an example. You are a role model for their future marriage.

WHERE DO WE FIGHT?

A woman asked me, "Then where *do* we fight?" This made me laugh. Well, the living room is a good place for heavy discussions, but inside your parked car offers you the ultimate seclusion, as it did for us one magnetic night in 1995.

It was the summer our family moved to Oahu, Hawaii. We left

our home in California for Glenn's new job at the Honolulu Athletic Club, and we rented a small house near the most beautiful beach in the world—Kailua Beach. The kids were in kindergarten and second grade. We had been married eight years. It was and it wasn't as glamorous as it sounds. We really struggled that year.

After three months, Glenn left his job for an opportunity that was too-good-to-be-true, and it wasn't working out. Namely, his boss went to jail, the company folded, and Glenn was unemployed shortly thereafter. The company had to get rid of assets quickly and gave Glenn the company car—a Ford Bronco— in lieu of a paycheck with a "Good luck to you and goodbye."

We had just moved to one of the most expensive places on earth and now lived there without an income. Our savings account rapidly diminished. Our rent was $1,600 without utilities. We were fighting. We were stressed, uncertain about our future, worried, and strained. We had both been hunting for jobs, unsuccessfully. Our friends and families were all on the mainland, and for the first time, I experienced the isolation of living on an island. I considered moving back to California—without Glenn.

He was fed up with our fighting. We hadn't been physically close in a long while. The stress created a discord between us. There was a huge, ugly block between us, and neither of us knew how to get around it. Something was terribly wrong in our marriage, and it was frightening to feel that vulnerable. A turning point was on the horizon, but we didn't know it yet.

We had both had a tough day looking for jobs and met at home disappointed. It was a strange juxtaposition, living in paradise and being so unhappy. We decided to have a talk that evening after the children went to bed.

The beach house we rented had thin walls, and with two tanned little girls sleeping soundly in their beds, we decided to talk in the Bronco. I thought we would discuss the details of the demise of our marriage—the divorce. I began to shake inside a little. My heart literally physically hurt. We couldn't stand our pain any longer and just wanted it to disappear, thinking perhaps that divorce was a way to get rid of it. Even though we never said it, it was there … the option … hanging over us like doom.

As I opened the screen door in the early evening and stepped outside, barefoot, onto front the front porch, a warm, salty, tropical breeze blanketed me, and the sweet perfume from the plumeria tree in the front yard soothed me. I stepped onto the dewy grass decorated with white and yellow plumeria flowers and looked up at the endless midnight-blue sky sprinkled with a million stars and a low-hung crescent moon. I inhaled deeply and took it all in. I exhaled slowly and felt relaxed, almost happy. Then I took another deep breath and headed toward the Bronco where Glenn awaited.

Once inside the Bronco, we didn't talk. Glenn seemed to be in deep thought. He sat in silence and so did I, afraid of our own words. We peered out the front dash window, looking at our little beach house with a soft golden light glowing through the plantation windows. I knew Glenn was thinking of our family just then.

Unexpectedly, we kissed. Alone in the car on a balmy summer's eve, our problems subsided momentarily, and it almost seemed like we were on a date. We kissed again and a fierce passion of mixed emotions—fury, fear, and love—swept through us, like a tidal wave. We made intense love in the "bucking" Bronco. I'm not sure why such an explosive connection occurred between us that night—perhaps the Hawaiian gods had sweetened the air with love under their Hula moon. That night we turned toward each other instead of away. There was hope in that. Sometimes you just don't need words.

Begin your discussions with "I feel"

Rather than blaming and accusing your husband as in, "You do this," or "You don't do that," voice your concerns by stating how you feel. "I feel frustrated because …" "I feel hurt when …" This alleviates your husband wanting to respond by defending himself, and it will be easier for him to understand what you are feeling.

Timing

Only begin approaching a big issue when you know you will have the time to work on it. Often, you'll need an hour to reach the depth of an issue to first release it in the open and then discuss, compromise, and resolve it. Just as there are appropriate places to argue, there is also an appropriate time.

Problem management

This technique comes from Glenn and his decades of management experience with people at work and is applicable to navigating through your marriage. He says, "Don't come to me with a problem, without a solution." For example, if you are frustrated with your husband's lack of consideration in giving you some private time alone, then ask for a specific time duration (like Monday nights twice a month) just for you. This is undoubtedly more effective in solving your needs rather than complaining to your husband that you don't have any time for yourself.

Softening sentences and sandwiching sentences

When you've got something yucky to say to him, it is much nicer to say something positive first (softening sentence) before hitting him with the negative. Or say it in between two positive sentences (sandwiching the negative sentence in the middle) to cushion the blow. If you want to be happily married, you will need to solve problems without damaging his ego and your relationship. At first, I thought that using these techniques would be obvious, and so it wouldn't work. Nothing could be further from the truth. Glenn knows when I'm softening and sandwiching my sentences and appreciates the kind-hearted communication. The same goes for me when he needs to tell me something.

Here is an example of a softening sentence: "I really liked being on your arm at the dinner party last night. Your usual wit and charm were alive. But, I felt uncomfortable when you asked the host how much he paid for his house." This is preferable to blurting out "I cannot believe you asked Dick how much he paid for his house. You embarrassed me."

Here is an example of sandwiching positive sentences in between a negative one: "Honey, thank you for power washing the side of the house. It looks so much better. But, could you please use less pressure because the paint is starting to chip off. I love having you home this afternoon, helping out. We're having your favorite, Proscuitto Wrapped Scallops, for dinner."

Prosciutto Wrapped Scallops

Prep time: 10 minutes
Cook time: 4 minutes
Serves: 4 to 6

6 slices prosciutto
12 medium size scallops
Juice of 1 lemon
Salt
Freshly ground pepper
2 tablespoons chopped chives
Toothpicks

Preheat your oven to broil.
Cut the prosciutto into four-inch long strips. Toss the scallops with the lemon juice, salt, pepper, and half of the chives. Wrap each scallop with a strip of prosciutto, securing with a toothpick. Place scallops upright on a lightly greased baking sheet.

Broil 2 minutes and turn them over. Broil another 2 minutes until the prosciutto is crispy. The scallops will continue to cook once out of the oven so be careful not to overcook them.

PRESENTATION
Place the scallops on a serving platter and sprinkle with the remaining fresh chopped chives. Serve immediately. A platter of sliced, ripe cantaloupe is a nice finish to the meal. Wine pairing: Pinot Noir or Petite Syrah.

These scallops are also terrific skewered and grilled on the BBQ. Spear five on a skewer interspersed with pineapple chunks, cherry tomatoes, onions, and peppers.

$\mathcal{R}$ole Changes
Letting go of gender stigmas

$\mathcal{M}$arriage is much like a dramatic play. There are many scenes and many acts. You will wear different costumes and change hats during its production. A mutual understanding between you and your husband regarding who plays what role in the marriage and when is fundamental. Remain flexible and be willing to change roles by letting go of gender stigmatism and stereotypes. Choose roles that utilize your personal strengths and allow you to contribute to the team in the best way that makes you happy. When the partners are happy in their roles, the team becomes strong, and the marriage functions well.

Act one, scene one. Glenn and I had been married three years. Incorrectly and naively, at the beginning of our marriage, I thought that each partner should contribute to the responsibilities of our lives 50/50. I figured (note that I didn't say we communicated) that we would each contribute evenly around the house, financially, and with the children. I assumed our roles would be equal. After all, I was raised in the 70s, and women's liberation was my birthright. It didn't occur to me that this liberation was still under construction and that the backlash included confused roles and a new perceived liberation called divorce.

I've learned that the contribution balance in marriage is sometimes way off. It could be 40/60 or 99/1 or, worse, 30/30. But equilibrium prevails in the long run, and roles change over time.

Those first years of marriage were out of balance. It was harder and more complicated than I thought. The sharing of responsibilities did not match what I had envisioned. I did 98 percent of the childrearing, cooking, and housework. He made 98 percent of the money. It seemed old fashioned—Glenn going off to work each morning, while I stayed home all day. I was college educated, and we had two mortgages to pay. The financial responsibility on Glenn was enormous, and I felt guilty not helping him out.

The physical demands of caring for a toddler and an infant were challenging for me, and Glenn wasn't happy to come home to a wife full of unmet expectations who changed diapers all day. Yet my heart longed to stay at home with my daughters. It was confusing. I was disillusioned. I was torn. Had I realized how short-lived these roles are and how quickly time ticks by, I would have accepted them, knowing that they would change. The roles you play in the revolving scenes of your life ought to be enjoyed to the fullest.

Act two, scene two. We had been married eight years. We changed roles. Glenn stayed home full time, raising our daughters, while I worked full time, climbing a management ladder. He bonded with our daughters in a way that many fathers don't get an opportunity to do. He coached our eldest daughter's baseball team (no, not softball), and she played right alongside the other boys on the team. He taught our youngest daughter to ride a bike and took both of them to the beach, almost daily.

They have fond memories of that time. It was precious to all three of them. He was the dad who packed their lunches, tied their shoes, and took them to elementary school. He was the dad who picked them up after school, while many of their friends went to day care. He was the dad who hugged them when they fell down, drove them to the orthodontist, helped them with their homework, and made them dinner. He was the dad who let them "veg out" in front of the TV while he folded the laundry. And he was the dad who started their baths while I worked late in the evening. He was incredible. The time he spent with the girls as their primary caregiver bonded their relationships for life. Our daughters adore him.

He bonded their relationship for life and our daughters adore him.

Act three, scene three. We had been married fifteen years, when we changed roles again. We own a business together, and we have defined new roles for ourselves within our business and our marriage. At home our roles could be considered traditional, until you look a little closer. Glenn mows the lawn, and I cook. Is this sexist? Old fashioned? Stereotypical? We don't think so. We chose these roles. I hate mowing the lawn, and Glenn loves to. He smokes a fat cigar while riding that big red thing with a beer in the cup holder—oh, brother. Very macho. While he's out in the yard sometimes I'll put on a dress (and lipstick) in anticipation of our family Sunday night dinner. Very feminine. This kind of scene might seem trite and boring to some, but not to us.

When I've got Baked Potato Cheese Soup pre-baking in the oven, I'll flip open my laptop, power up the Wi-Fi, and scan the latest real estate listings on the Web—hunting for our next investment and crunching numbers in my head as I cook, happily fulfilled in my multiple roles.

Roles for women and men should be defined as uniquely as their marriages. Throughout a long love life of a good marriage, there are phases—many scenes and many acts. They do not last. Accept them for what they are at the moment and strive toward a workable balance by communicating your needs and compromising to meet his.

Baked Potato Cheese Soup (v)

Half potato/half cheese … a good balance

Prep time: 20 minutes
Cook time: 1 hour
Serves: 6 to 8 (You'll want leftovers and the soup freezes well.)

3 large russet potatoes, quartered and partially peeled
2 medium sweet onions, quartered
3 large carrots, scrubbed and cut into large chunks
¼ cup melted butter
5 cups chicken or vegetable stock
A handful fresh parsley, chopped
1 tablespoon dried dill
1¼ cup grated cheddar cheese
1¼ cup grated Monterey jack cheese
Salt
Freshly ground pepper

Preheat your oven to 350°F.
By leaving part or all of the skin on the potatoes and carrots you add more nutrients to your soup. In a large mixing bowl toss the potatoes, onions, and carrots with the melted butter, salt, and pepper. Transfer to a baking pan and bake for 30 minutes.

Meanwhile, warm the stock in a large pot on the stove. After baking, add the potatoes, onions, carrots, parsley, and dill to the stock. Cook on medium-low heat for about 10 minutes until the potatoes and carrots are very soft. Let it cool 15 minutes. Puree the soup with your magic wand right in the pot. Sprinkle in grated cheeses, a little at a time, melting the cheese slowly. Add more salt and pepper to taste.

PRESENTATION
Serve with a loaf of crusty, fresh baked bread and apple wedges.

$\mathcal{M}$arriage Maintenance

You've got to work at it

$\mathcal{M}$aintaining your marriage is a daily devotion. The world moves very quickly. Change can happen in an hour. Moods swing and shift, almost unnoticed, unless you are paying attention.

Be connected with the intricate details of your husband's life. Take interest in him and offer small gestures. For example: "I was thinking of you today wearing that blue shirt and how nice you look in it." And, of course, back him up with big events: "I support you and your decision to decline that offer." He must know you are there by his side, even when you are not physically there. He needs you listening as a companion, cheering like a cheerleader, keeping a secret as a confidant, and supporting him as a friend. Be his best friend, his life partner, his nest maker, and his wife.

Who is the first person he thinks of calling when he lands an account at work? Not his assistant, I hope. Will he think of you during a business lunch at a new restaurant and call you from his cell because he can't wait to tell you about the eggplant parmesan? Does he want to take you there? Are you the woman he wants to see when he's having a bad day because he needs cheering up, and you're just the girl to do it? Are you the woman he wants to see if he's having a great day and wants to continue it with you? Go have the eggplant parmesan.

While living in a closely connected happy marriage filled with love, laughter, and support, there is little room for negative thoughts of temptation, a wandering eye, or the dreaded—infidelity. Maintaining your marriage daily won't allow for decay, which can begin subtly—

little by little, day by day. It begins with neglect and the mistake of not placing the importance of the relationship as a priority in life's daily activities. At first, the negligence can hardly be felt, then it becomes slightly disappointing, then you settle, accepting it as the norm, and then it's tolerated—begrudgingly. Finally, you both can't ignore that there's a void, and you are now both vulnerable to negative thoughts.

Don't take your marriage for granted. You've heard it before: You've got to work at it. Here's a marriage maintenance checklist:

M - Most important relationship
A - Action (take action daily for it)
R - Resolve problems daily
R - Responsible for it—you are
I - Involved
A - Attitude of love and gratitude
G - Guts to stick it out
E - Eager for each other and its success

I've got a good-looking, charismatic husband. Throughout the years, many women have hit on Glenn in the most forward of ways. One woman (a customer—or perhaps she could be called a stalker) was so aggressive that upon learning that Glenn had been promoted and transferred, she tracked him down at his new job location, walked right up to him at work, and asked him to step outside with her. Then she blatantly asked him if he was happily married. She proceeded to tell him that she was not happily married and wondered if he would like to have an affair.

Several other women have telephoned his co-workers to ask if he was married. Another brazen female called him on the phone at work, described her body in detail, and asked him to come over to her house to pour caramel sauce over her breast implants and photograph her nude so she could send the pictures to *Playboy* magazine. Two women, after a couple of glasses of wine, have privately "confessed" *to me* their crushes on my husband. Even our teenage daughters have friends who think their dad is "hot" and would date him.

Glenn sends out the signal "I'm taken." He wears a wedding ring. He is flattered by the attention and tells me about it when it happens.

I momentarily get a twinge of panic, but it doesn't last long. I am maintaining my marriage daily, even hourly. I know our bond is tight. I'm meeting him today for lunch at the new restaurant to taste their eggplant parmesan. I doubt it is as good as mine!

Eggplant Parmesan (v)

Prep time: 1 hour
Cook time: 30 minutes
Serves: 4 to 6

MAIN DISH
2 eggplants
1 tablespoon sea salt
½ cup olive oil
A handful of fresh basil, chopped
A handful of fresh Italian parsley, chopped
1 egg, whisked
½ cup heavy cream
2 cups grated mozzarella cheese
2 cups ricotta cheese
1 cup parmesan cheese
Tomato Medley (recipe below)
½ cup of red wine (if desired)

Make a batch of Tomato Medley (recipe follows), add the red wine, and simmer it on low heat for 15 minutes to create a fresh, homemade chunky tomato sauce.

Preheat your oven to 350°F.
Cut off the ends of the eggplants and discard them. Hold the eggplant upright and peel a few long thick strips of skin off the eggplant, removing a strip of skin about every other inch. (It will look striped.) Slice the eggplants about ¼ inch thick. Sprinkle them with sea salt and lay them out individually on a baking sheet for 30 minutes to draw out excess moisture. Rinse the salt off the eggplant slices, dry them, and baste both sides with olive oil. Return them to a clean baking sheet and bake about 15 minutes, until they are soft and turning dark.

While the eggplant is in the oven, fold together, in a mixing bowl, the herbs, egg, heavy cream, and cheeses.

Remove the eggplant from the oven. You are now ready to layer. In a medium-sized baking dish, spread some Tomato Medley sauce on the bottom of the dish. Then layer in the following order: eggplant slice, ¼ cup of sauce, ¼ cup of cheese mixture, and repeat, overlapping your eggplant slices as you go. Use the back of a spoon to help you spread the sauce and cheese mixture evenly. Pour any remaining sauce and cheese mixture over the top.

Cover with foil and bake at 350°F for 20 minutes. Remove the foil and let it brown 10 more minutes. It will be bubbling.

Tomato Medley (v)

Choose a combination of three or more of your favorite tomatoes, but they must be perfectly ripe. We like to use vine-ripened heirloom tomatoes whenever our budget allows. But a combination of grape, cherry, and roma tomatoes make a great medley, too.

Prep time: 10 minutes
Cook time: None

2 cups of chopped fresh tomatoes
3 tablespoons extra virgin olive oil
1 tablespoon balsamic vinegar
1 clove fresh garlic, minced
1 cup fresh basil, chopped
Salt
Freshly ground pepper

Combine all ingredients together in a bowl. That's it! Tomato Medley is wonderful served fresh (without simmering). It can be tossed with pasta, put on toasted baguettes (bruschetta), used as a fresh pizza topping, or served on top of salads.

Tomato Medley simmered on low for 15 minutes becomes a delicious homemade marinara sauce for eggplant Parmesan, pizzas, and pastas.

PRESENTATION
Allow the Eggplant Parmesan to rest 10 minutes before serving. Garnish with a sprinkling of fresh chopped basil and Italian parsley.

Honey Do

"You're the man!"

*Y*our husband wants to please you, but, poor guy, he often doesn't know how. Before Glenn and I learned these communication techniques, he usually felt that he either didn't do what I asked the right way or at the right time or worse, he simply forgot to do it. Regretfully, I would start to nag, and I resented having to remind myself to remind him to remember, acting as a mother figure—not as a wife. Glenn thought I was difficult to please. If this type of rut sounds familiar to you, read on.

For your husband's "honey do" projects, remember these important truths. Husbands need our help in order for them to please us. They are not mind readers, and they feel frustrated because we change our minds frequently. They do not know what we want at any given moment or at the grocery store. They do not think like us, and they prefer to focus on a single project at a time—they do not like to multitask. Use the following communication tools for a smooth accomplishment of minor tasks. These tools are excellent for him to use with you, as well, when he asks you to do something.

GROCERY STORE LIST:

*W*rite exactly what he needs to buy: Don't write just the word "yeast," instead write:

One packet of active dry yeast (located in the baking section).

This way, you get what you want, and he doesn't have to guess at what you really want.

PERSONAL SCHEDULE LIST:

Write out, in detail, what you would like him to do. For example:

Pick up daughter 3 PM. Bring her a healthy snack and a water bottle.
Take her to horseback riding, which starts at 4 PM (her gear is in the back of the car).
Be home by 6:30 PM for our dinner party and please pick up our favorite red wine (Hirsch Pinot Noir) to go with the homemade pizzas.
Love u.

HONEY DO LIST:

When you ask him to help you, value your husband's time by giving a definite completion to the tasks. They don't like to feel that you have an endless list for them. Once they are finished with the task don't add on more. Also, let him do the project on his own. Husbands don't like to feel that you are watching their every move. They like to do the chores in their own time frame, in their own way. Sometimes it's a good idea to leave for the day and let him putter around the house on his own. You can leave him a simple note similar to this:

Clean rain gutters.
Fix upstairs hall closet door.
Thank you honey, the rest of the day is yours, have fun!
See you later.
Love, me.

REPEAT BACK:

When you ask him to do something, as a courtesy to you, ask your husband to repeat it back to you in his own words, so you know you've been heard or understood. For example, he'd say, "Good morning honey, I got your note. I'm going to clean the rain gutters and fix the closet door, then I'm off to play basketball." This way you are both satisfied and can expect the day to unfold as agreed, happily.

FOLLOW THROUGH:

*W*hen the task is complete, again, as a courtesy to you, ask your husband to tell you the job is done. "Honey, the closet door is fixed, and the rain gutters are clean. We are ready for a storm. I'm off to the gym now to work off the pizza." This way you won't be tempted to nag by asking, "Did you clean the rain gutters yet?" which may increase your husband's frustration if the job is not yet finished.

WOMEN NEED TO FEEL THEY HAVE SUPPORT:

*W*hen you are exasperated (close to the boiling point), ask your husband to say, "How can I help you, honey?" That simple phrase takes the load off immediately and has such promise and support. I love this phrase, and my children also say to me, "How can I help you, mama?" It's music to my ears.

When they ask this simple question, my mood changes. I feel supported and not alone in a whirlwind of overwhelming tasks. My voice softens; I kindly delegate; and everyone is happier. I'd say to my daughter, "I have a fun project for you. Would you please knead the pizza dough and fold in the little rosemary leaves?"

MEN NEED TO FEEL THEY HAVE A PURPOSE:

*M*en identify themselves by their work. Men need and want a purpose, a task, a job to do—something to wake up for. It is as simple as that. It doesn't matter if he completed a corporate merger today or if he changed the oil in the car. His need to be recognized as a "capable and productive man" is similar.

MEN NEED TO BE THANKED:

As equally important as the task is an acknowledgment, by you, of his accomplishing it. Husbands need and want this appreciation—and lots of it.

They take pride in their work and want you to notice. Acknowledge his contribution to your life with positive reinforcements like: "I really appreciate you taking the time to buy this fabulous wine. I love it." "Thank you for going to the grocery store. You really took the edge off my afternoon." "You have real pride in your work. It shows. I am so thankful that you take such good care of our home." "It is important to me that our home looks nice. Thank you for cleaning the rain gutters." "We have a well maintained home. All wives should be so lucky. You are handy." "Thank you for saving us money by cleaning those gutters. You deserve the afternoon off. Go watch the game. I'll bring you a couple slices of leftover pizza." "You're the man!"

Homemade Pizzas (v)

This simple recipe for pizza crusts allows for many options.
Blend interesting ingredients into the dough and switch toppings by
using leftovers or what you've got on hand.

CRUST

Prep time: 20 minutes (and an additional 1 hour for the pizza dough
to rise)
Cook time: 20 minutes

1 packet active dry yeast
½ cups lukewarm water
1 large pinch sugar (brown sugar can be used if you like)
1 teaspoon salt
2 tablespoons olive oil
2½ cups all purpose flour, plus ½ cup for kneading the dough
¼ cup corn meal
Sea salt
Freshly ground pepper

Preheat your oven to 425°F.
In a large bowl dissolve the yeast in the lukewarm water, add the sugar,
and let it rest 10 minutes. Then stir in the salt, olive oil, and 2½ cups
of flour.

Next, heavily flour a board and knead the dough about 10 times, folding
in your crust additions, if desired. Return the dough back to the bowl
greased with a little olive oil to prevent sticking. Cover it with a tea towel
and let it sit at room temperature for an hour.

When it has risen to twice its size, punch it down (husbands love to do
this) and make a ball. Then roll the dough out on your floured board,
making your desired pizza shape. Before adding toppings, brush a little
more olive oil on the bottom of the pizza pan and sprinkle the pan with

corn meal (this gives the bottom of the pizza a nice crunch). Lastly, brush the top of the pizza with olive oil and sprinkle it with sea salt and freshly ground pepper. Add your desired toppings and bake about 20 minutes.

CRUST ADDITIONS

Optional choices for folding into the crust: A handful of fresh minced or roasted garlic, fresh rosemary, chopped basil or Italian parsley leaves, grated parmesan or romano cheese, red pepper flakes, caramelized onions.

Two of our favorite "flat breads" using the pizza crust recipe:
Rosemary Flatbread: Blend into the dough a handful of fresh, chopped rosemary. Roll the dough thin and top with shaved parmesan cheese before baking. It bakes in 10 minutes. Serve with soups or salads or as a complement to main dishes. We also make sandwiches with it.

Roasted Garlic & Onion Flatbread: Blend into the dough a few tablespoons of mashed roasted garlic and 1 cup of thinly sliced caramelized red onions. (Cut the top off of a whole head of garlic and bake it 30 minutes in a 350°F oven. Caramelize 2 cups of sliced red onions with 2 tablespoons of butter in a saucepan over low heat for 40 minutes. It will reduce to 1 cup.)

PIZZA TOPPINGS

Tomato medley, fresh mozzarella, and shaved parmesan.
Prosciutto and pineapple.
Small morsels of Italian sausage, fresh basil, and spinach leaves with sliced roma tomatoes.
Shredded roasted chicken, sliced green onions, chopped cilantro, and Thai chili sauce.
Tiny fresh mozzarella balls, shrimp, capers, and very thin slices of zucchini and red onions.
Crumbled feta, chopped olives, and chopped fresh basil.

LOVE

Manners

Knock, knock

The definition of polite is showing regard for others in manners and speech. Strive for that in your marriage. And never underestimate the power of a please and thank you. There is a unique balance in a marriage of being comfortable and being polite. I recommend living more on the polite side.

I've heard of couples that use the bathroom in front of each other and perform other personal grooming habits without the slightest regard for whether or not their spouse is in the room. Frankly, there are some things that are better kept private! Exiting the bathroom "all clean and shiny" is very attractive, if you ask me. Why in the world couples let down their guard so that all is revealed I will never know. Of course, when partners are sick or feeling kind of slouchy, things might slip a bit. Or, at dinner at home together, one of you might do something that is quite rude, but just keep working at finding that balance of being comfortable and being polite.

One Sunday morning I rose to an empty bed. I wondered, *where's Glenn?* When getting my coffee in the kitchen, I could hear Le Tour de France on the guest bedroom television, and I realized he considerately had gone in there to watch the bike race and let me slumber. *Nice,* I thought. Then I walked toward the guest room to say good morning.

The bedroom door was only slightly ajar, so I knocked. I waited a few seconds, until he said, "Come in." When I entered, I saw that he was snuggled up under the comforter drinking his morning cup of coffee. He smiled and said, "It is nice that you knocked." This is how we began another day together, with a slight smile toward each other on a regular morning. It really is the little things in a marriage that count. The simple considerate act of knocking on a door shows your spouse respect. Manners are a shining example of that.

I left the door as I found it, slightly ajar, and returned to the kitchen to make us a lovely breakfast that I brought back to him in bed. Still wearing my robe and precariously holding a large teak-wood serving tray with a just out-of-the oven Orange Currant Nutmeg Scones, scrambled eggs, and fresh squeezed orange juice, I again knocked, but this time with my foot. "Knock. Knock."

Orange Currant Nutmeg Scones

I usually get an extra hug when I pop these scones out of the oven.
It is quite possible to get your husband to fall in love with you all over
again by intoxicating him with these baking aromas.

Prep time: 15 minutes
Cook time: 20 minutes
Serves: 4

2 cups flour
$^1/_3$ cup sugar
2 teaspoons baking powder
¼ teaspoon salt
¼ cup cold butter, cut into small pieces
¼ cup shortening
½ teaspoon nutmeg
¾ cup currants
½ teaspoon finely grated orange peel
1 egg whisked
¼ cup milk

Preheat your oven to 350°F.
In a large bowl combine flour, sugar, baking powder, and salt. Cut the butter and shortening into the dry ingredients with a pastry cutter (or you may use two dinner knives) until the mixture is crumbly. Using a fork, stir in the remaining ingredients.

Knead the dough on a floured surface six times, folding it over each time. Roll out the dough ½ inch thick and cut into desired shapes using cookie cutters.

Or to make traditional triangular scones, roll dough into a large ½-inch thick circle and cut crosswise 4 times to make 8 scones. Bake it as a whole 20 minutes on a greased baking sheet until the tops are golden. Separate the triangles when cooled.

PRESENTATION

Every Christmas morning I bake these scones and serve them warm in a
basket lined with a fresh tea towel and with a cup of raspberry preserves
holding a tiny spoon. We eat them while opening our presents.

Appreciation
The little things add up

What are you grateful for? When did you last take the time to have a moment of appreciation for everything you have, especially your husband? I believe you should do this privately, every day. Oh, but don't we girls know how easy it is to get on an opposite negative roll? I know of women who call each other up for daily venting sessions on the telephone. They run through the worn out list of their respective, repetitive annoyances. I've done this myself and found that when I hang up the phone I feel worse, not better; I don't feel relieved, but instead, depressed. I also know of a women's group where the members get together weekly to knit and call their gatherings "Bitch and Stitch!" Let's stop this, ladies.

If you let them, the list of things you don't appreciate about your husband can grow and destroy your marriage. After years of married life together, some regrets and resentments may find their way into your thoughts, and they can build up. You will undoubtedly say to yourself at some point, "I wish he was more …" However, this kind of negative thinking gets you nowhere. Focusing on your list of have not will only leave you without. Without a husband, that is.

Instead, think about what you do appreciate about your husband. The little things add up. Glenn removes his shoes before coming in the house. He brought home a chick flick last night for us to watch, when I know he'd rather see *The Matrix* for the fourth time. He spent his week's vacation and his quarterly bonus check on replacing the decks instead of going on that California trip with his high school buddies a few summers ago.

One time, when I wasn't in an appreciative mood, I made myself write down the most important qualities I really appreciated about Glenn. Once I finished, everything else that was bugging me at that moment paled in comparison and still does. I keep the list in a journal in my nightstand next to our bed. I read it. I add to it. It helps to keep myself in check and remember what is really important and how much I really appreciate him. If I'm asked whether my glass is half empty or half full, I love to reply, "My cup runneth over." I remind myself several times a day—upon waking, driving in the car, at bed time … anytime.

I practice making the choice to have a good attitude. I also tell Glenn in private and in front of others what I appreciate about him. It builds his confidence, and he knows I value him. I share with you, right out of my journal, my ever-growing list of love for Glenn, for who he is.

Charismatic
Resourceful
Handy
Kind
Creative
Technical
Magnetic
Determined
Handsome
A good father
Empowered
Quiet
An incredible lover
Humorous
Peaceful
Helpful
Loving
Hardworking
Considerate

Affectionate
Allowing
Educated
Accepting
Wise
Willing
Risk taker
My best friend
Trustworthy
Athletic
Careful
Sincere
Team Player
Happy-go-lucky
Respectful
Communicator
Stable
Tolerant
Artistic
Committed
Insightful
Funny
Reliable
Light hearted
Patient
Original
Honest
Intelligent
Entrepreneur
Respected
Loyal
Boyish
Agreeable
Friendly
Loves me

What you project outward comes back to you in droves, and this was exemplified to me on Mother's Day of 2008. Glenn validated how much he appreciates me by a simple act of love, but in turn, this became the night I appreciated him most.

I was having mixed feelings alternating between thankfulness that I was a mother and sadness that my nest was now empty. Our little birds had flown off to college—literally—and this year was the first time that the four of us would not be together on Mother's Day. Our youngest wouldn't be with us that day, but our eldest would be.

I pouted around the house all morning. I couldn't think of what I wanted to do for Mother's Day. I pondered, *should we go out to brunch? Nah. Go for a walk in Forest Park? No, I don't really feel like it. Pore over our family photo albums and weep for days gone by? That's probably not a good idea. Put on a happy face for our eldest daughter? Yes, I'll do that.* But, there was a void I could not fill.

I'm not a person usually inclined to be an "emotional" eater, turning to food for comfort. I pride myself on my nutritional choices and portion control. However, while sitting alone pondering how I could improve my mood, I had the most wonderful idea of indulging in a caloric feast of Papa's Fried Chicken. I had to have it!

Glenn had recently opened Café Reese, and because it was a new business, I didn't think I'd see him much that day, as he was striving for his success in the marketplace. Perhaps, he, too, was trying to fill the void of our empty nest through his new "baby," the restaurant. So, I decided to make Papa's Fried Chicken and began distracting my sorry-self with the shopping list.

At 4:00 PM Glenn called and said he just closed the restaurant and was coming home to make me dinner. "What do you want?" he asked. "Papa's fried chicken!" I gushed, excitedly. Our eldest daughter arrived shortly thereafter, and the three of us cooked for more than an hour, listening to the chicken sizzle; boiling potatoes and whipping them with sour cream, roasted garlic, and chives; sautéing collard greens; steaming corn on the cob and drizzling it with butter, salt, and pepper; and finally, with much anticipation, making the gravy.

We happily devoured every morsel on our plates, appreciating a southern feast we seldom allow ourselves to indulge in, and we knew it would be this good. It was satisfying and worth the mess.

The next morning at Café Reese a tall and beautiful woman with short, bobbed red hair and green eyes requested to meet me. She had come by the café the evening before for a glass of wine and was surprised to see that we were closed. When she heard why, she wanted to meet the woman who could get her husband to close his restaurant to make her fried chicken. She walked right up to me, smiled, looked me in the eye, and shook my hand.

Papa's Fried Chicken

Papa (Glenn's father, named Reese) would set the chicken on low and go out to work in the yard. He could hear the crackling oil from outside and knew when it was time to turn the chicken. He would call into the house from the yard, "Babe, turn the chicken!"

Prep time: 10 minutes
Cook time: 45 minutes
Serves: 4 to 6

4 to 6 servings of chicken (skin on and bone in)
2 cups all purpose flour
Salt
Freshly ground pepper
Corn oil for frying

FOUR SECRETS TO PAPA'S FRIED CHICKEN

1. The secret to the crisp is to wash the chicken and toss it into the flour mixture when the chicken is very wet. The flour sticks.
2. Put the lid on three-quarters of the way to cook the inside.
3. Turn the chicken only once.
4. Let it drain and cool on a platter of paper towels. Then salt it.

In a large plastic bag, combine the flour and salt and pepper and set aside. Wash the chicken pieces but do not dry them. Toss the chicken into the flour mixture when the chicken is very wet and shake it in the bag. This gets the flour to stick.

Next, pour corn oil—about 1½ inches deep—into the bottom of a large frying pan. Heat until very hot. The chicken should crackle and bubble vigorously when you submerge it. Once the chicken is in the pan and bubbling, turn the heat to low and put the lid on three-quarters of the way so that the inside cooks through in about 45 minutes.
Turn the chicken only once, halfway through frying.

Once golden and crispy, remove the chicken and let it cool on a large platter lined with paper towels. Then salt it.

Honor Your Spouse's Family

Big Mama is watching

In-laws! For better or for worse, they are your spouse's kin. Have the patience and the courage to step out lovingly toward them. Welcome your spouse's family into your home. Cook for them. Take their calls and happily talk to them. Throw parties in their honor. Take them out to eat. Send cards, gifts … the whole shebang. When you honor your spouse's family, you are actually honoring your spouse. Invoke your most gracious self in the midst of interesting interpersonal relations and wholeheartedly accept your husband's family, as I did.

My mother-in-law, Virginia, and her mother, Big Mama, and Big Mama's sister, Wawa, were all born in Manila, Philippines. Glenn's father, Reese, is an American born in South Dakota. Reese asked Virginia to dance at a military party in the Philippines in 1953 when he was stationed there during the Korean War. They married, and he moved her to South Dakota when she was just seventeen years old. They moved to California, raised a family, and were married thirty-six years before Reese passed away.

My initiation into Glenn's Filipino family was a bit of a mishap. It was a sticky, hot, windless summer afternoon in Los Angeles. The year was 1987. Glenn and I were newly engaged and pregnant. We had been driving south, in the miserable heat, for seven hours from San Francisco to LA, so I could meet his family. I was nauseous most of the time and weak. I was suffering from morning sickness that lasted all day, every day. I could hardly keep anything down. Intermittently, I could suck on saltine crackers. Finally, we arrived at Glenn's Aunt Wawa's house on Dillon Street in our white Toyota Corolla.

Glenn opened the front door without knocking, and we entered a small house filled with card tables and about thirty Filipino men and women playing mahjong. It was a Filipino casino in full force in the middle of the day. Wawa was running a profitable side business in the house. A cloud of cigarette smoke almost knocked me out. The sounds of the mahjong tiles clicking together combined with the sound of Tagalog spoken very rapidly were astounding. Then lots of women and men immediately started shouting "Glenn, Glenn!" and hugs and tears surrounded him. I was standing alone, mesmerized. After all of the commotion, we were ushered to the back of the house to see Big Mama.

As we walked through a small kitchen, we passed huge pots of chicken adobo cooking on the stove with women tending to them. Garlic and vinegar vapors permeated the air. We were seated at the back breakfast nook where Big Mama awaited us. She didn't say a word to me. I was intimidated. All of the windows were closed. The smells triggered more nausea, and I suddenly felt very hot. I looked at Glenn for reassurance. He smiled. More Tagalog was spoken, and several large cooked crabs were placed on the center of the Formica table.

While Big Mama sat, she silently and rhythmically dipped three fingertips full of rice into a small dish of vinegar and then into her mouth. These customs and table manners were uncomfortably new to me. I didn't know what to do with myself. I have never felt so out of place in my life, and, yet, I liked it there.

I felt the love and the closeness of his family. I saw how much they all loved Glenn and missed him. I saw how much he loved them. I was in awe of this closeness. Wawa helped raised Glenn, and he had lived in that home as a child. I knew that Big Mama had fed dozens of children in the family, including Glenn, with those fingertips, with the babe perched on her lap. I wanted Big Mama to feed our unborn child in this way one day. And so I, too, sat in silence, respecting, appreciating, and accepting my husband's family and a culture completely different from mine.

My initiation into the family began when Big Mama took a cooked female crab, turned it over and opened up the shell (with her bare hands) and offered me the coveted crab eggs. But, at the time, not only was I nauseously pregnant, I was a vegetarian. There was silence after Glenn explained why I could not eat the eggs. No one in the room could understand why I would not accept Big Mama's offering of the eggs. Aunts and friends in the kitchen began speaking Tagalog very quickly, and then I heard the word "vegetarian" spoken in English bounce off their lips, awkwardly. The women looked at me oddly and nodded and then looked down. Big Mama kept eating her rice.

I really felt sick at this point, partly because of nerves but mostly because of the smells. I excused myself to the bathroom. It wasn't a great initiation. In hindsight, I would have accepted the crab eggs and honored Glenn's family.

I have, however, come to love Filipino Adobo and the way its simmering aromas fondly remind Glenn of his family. I think I'll make it for him tonight.

Filipino Adobo

*M*y in-laws insist on serving white rice with their adobo, so don't even think about substituting brown rice. Glenn's family recipe for making rice is a time-honored tradition. Whoever prepares the rice dips their middle finger into the bottom of a rice cooker and uses the lines on their finger to measure the water level to the proportion of rice at the bottom. They have shown me how to do this many times, but I still don't get it. I am stuck with the incongruous idea that everyone's hand is a different size, and, therefore, it won't be consistent. I am mistaken, apparently, because their rice comes out perfectly every time, regardless of who measures.

The first year we were married I went through Glenn's bachelor belongings while he was at work (big new wife mistake), and I got rid of two electric rice cookers because I didn't know what they were used for. He was furious. I begged him not to tell my mother-in-law for fear of being ostracized from the family, and he never did.

Prep time: 10 minutes
Cook time: 40 minutes
Serves: 6 to 8 (You'll want leftovers.)

6–8 servings of chicken (skin on and bone in)
1 bay leaf
Lots of crushed garlic—"that's the trick," says my mother-in-law—about 6 cloves
3 cups soy sauce
1 cup red wine vinegar
1 tablespoon whole peppercorns
8 cups white rice

Follow the package directions to make the rice or make it as my in-laws do.
Bring all other ingredients to a boil in a large pot. Boil for 10 minutes. Turn down heat to low and simmer, covered for 30 minutes. Strain the sauce to remove the bay leaf and the peppercorns.

PRESENTATION

Serve Filipino Adobo from your kitchen stove. I love seeing my friends and family lined up peering over each other's shoulders eagerly waiting their turn at the stove to receive their adobo, while I ladle out the chicken and lots of the sauce over the white rice. Naturally, I came to serve it this way, as Glenn's family does.

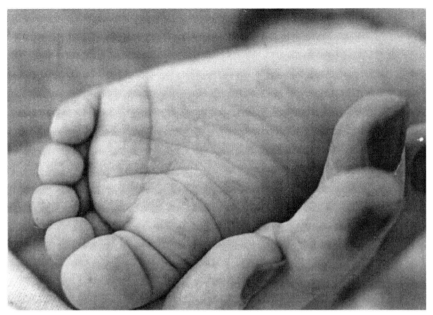

One of life's greatest gifts ... children. My hand
holding my youngest daughter's newborn foot.

Parenting

Now your marriage is twofold

No other experience will affect your marriage quite like deciding to become (or accidentally becoming) parents.

Ideally, the two of you would be great friends before getting married, have had several years to create flourishing careers, have traveled extensively, have purchased a lovely four-bedroom home with plenty of room for a nursery, have a jungle gym planned for the backyard, and have tens of thousands of dollars in the bank so one of you could stay home full time. Ha! As we all know, life is not usually quite this ideal.

Becoming parents with this ideal scene would be stressful enough. Add in the reality of juggling day care; working two or three jobs to pay the rent, the car payment, and the credit card bills; combined with diminished sleep and reduced disposable income, and you have a recipe for trouble. Your marriage will likely take the brunt of it.

On the positive side, however, you and your husband will be uniting in a very important and meaningful way. You will be enjoying one of life's greatest gifts: children. With the embracement of this new role you must carve out time for the two of you without the children. You must place your marriage as paramount to all other responsibilities, including the children, and become leaders of your family. Your strong marital bond should blanket and comfort the new souls entrusted to your care. Your children will hear, see, remember, and probably emulate most of your patterns.

Now your marriage is twofold: the couple and the parents. There is distinction. Both are alive and important entities. Embrace and nurture them both. Actively, purposefully, and routinely make time for each entity. Keep the spark alive for the couple and lead the family as parents. It's a life challenge. It's a marital challenge, but you can rise up to its rewards and the results are definitely worth it.

I've met several middle-aged divorced women who had let their marriages slip away during child rearing. About ten years ago a woman I barely knew told me that after the last child had left the house, she looked at her husband blankly and thought, *is this all that's left?* It seemed to me that she had forgotten about him a long time ago. In that moment, I determined to do it differently. I certainly didn't want to be just like her one day.

Just recently, I observed a frowning young mother at a park with two toddlers under foot. She was bossing her brow-beaten, unsmiling husband around as if he were her third toddler, and I thought, *oh, I wish she could stand back and see herself. Was this their family time at the park?*

Uniquely and simultaneously cultivate your marriage and your kids. Both will develop and grow. Perhaps you and your husband can't go out to dinner as often, but you could have date night number two—star gazing (summer's eve on the lawn; bring blankets, pillows, binoculars, cherries, chocolates, and Pinot Noir). The next morning play your song over chai tea, just before the kids get up. There you have created two dates back-to-back in the middle of the week, without hiring a sitter.

Don't wait for large chunks of time to connect. They will be few and far between. You've got to sneak in your moments. Say your terms of endearment to each other. ("Hi, Romeo." "Good morning, honey.")

Hug often. Share that secret look across the macaroni and cheese at the kitchen table, connecting for a moment, above the chaos of the kids. Don't forget the marriage because it is easy to put "us" on hold when what is really needed is for the two of you to hold on to "us." Strengthen your bond in small ways every single day during the roller coaster ride of child rearing.

Just after our first daughter was born, we drove from San Francisco to Southern California to present the "granddaughter" to the family. Glenn's parents had a big party for us at his family home. His brother, sister, their children, aunts, uncles, and friends all came to laugh, talk, drink, and eat with us. At 6:00 PM we put our baby daughter to bed. Swaddled tightly and sleeping soundly, we left her in Glenn's high school bedroom, where we were staying for the night.

Leaving the baby monitor on, we returned to the party, relaxing and enjoying ourselves in the kitchen—the heart of the party. We laughed and talked until midnight. Big Mama had gone to bed, and a few friends who were spending the night retired to bed too. Glenn and I wound down by watching TV with Glenn's mother in the family room that adjoins the kitchen. "Let's go to bed," Glenn suggested after awhile. We hugged his mom good night, leaving her to finish the TV show.

When I entered his old bedroom, a flirty curiosity came over me. "Was this really your high school bedroom?" I playfully asked, looking around.

"Yes," he replied.

"Did you ever sneak out the window at night?" I said as I lay down on the bed giving him my come hither look.

"Yes," he replied again with a question in his tone, wondering where this was going.

"Did you ever sneak a girlfriend in here at night?" I said, giving him a wink.

"Why do you want to know?" he said, while tickling me. We bantered back and forth, teasing each other, flirting. When things got heated, we put our daughter in the room next to his and then made passionate love.

Afterward, Glenn went to the kitchen for a couple of glasses of water and moved about quietly so as not to disturb his mother who had fallen asleep on the couch. While filling up our glasses at the sink, Glenn heard me cough, which curiously sounded as if I was in the kitchen with him. He turned around very slowly, dreading what he already knew, but had not yet confirmed—you guessed it—the baby monitor green light was on. It sat right where we left it on the kitchen counter, listening.

To this day, we are not sure whether anyone in the house—in particular, my mother-in-law—heard our passion broadcast over the monitor. Glenn thinks his mother was pretending to be asleep. We never asked. I still feel the weight of my embarrassment and remorse when I think about that discovery. He said all of the color left my face, and I turned white as a ghost when he came back to the bedroom with my glass of water and told me. After all, I was new to the family. We now share a secret look, remembering the mishap of the baby monitor every time we see one. Apparently they now have video camera baby monitors—beware!

And so we began our journey of marriage as parents, six months after saying "I do." We had to make the time for "us" along the way. It is not easy, nor is parenting, but anything worth having is worth the effort to achieve it.

Adult Macaroni and Cheese (v)

Kids like it too

Prep time: 5 minutes
Cook time: 15 minutes
Serves: 4 to 6

Improvise with cheeses you have on hand to discover new variations.

Five handfuls of hearty pasta noodles: rigatoni, penne, or ziti
2 tablespoons butter
1 tablespoon flour
Salt
Freshly ground pepper
1 cup whole milk or half-and-half (warmed)
1 handful of grated cheese (high-quality white cheddar)
1 handful of another variety of gourmet grated cheese (we like Gruyère)
A dash of nutmeg
A handful of shaved parmesan cheese for the topping
Two handfuls of steamed vegetables (if desired)

Boil the pasta in lots of salted water. Drain and put in a large bowl. Stir in 1 tablespoon of butter. Set aside. Using the same pot (who likes to do more dishes?), add the flour, salt, pepper, and the other tablespoon of butter. Stir on low heat, making a roux.

Slowly pour in the warmed milk or half-and-half and stir, forming a sauce. Add back the pasta and gently fold in the grated cheeses, slowly, a few sprinkles at a time, stirring the pasta as you go so the cheese melts evenly, and the pasta is ultimately coated with the creamy, cheesy sauce. Add a dash of nutmeg and additional salt and pepper to taste.

PRESENTATION

There is something quite satisfying about eating Mac and Cheese out of a bowl, with a spoon. Just before serving sprinkle each bowl with shaved Parmesan and top with steamed vegetables, if desired.

Sunday Night Dinner

Just be home by 5:00

*I*nsist on it. No matter who's asking, who they are with, or where they are going, on Sunday morning say, "Okay, honey, just be home by 5:00 for Sunday night dinner." This goes for husbands as well as kids. Commit to it and say it every week.

It does not matter who cooks Sunday night dinner, although everyone joining in to help is ideal, and it does not matter what you have to eat or whether it takes three hours or fifteen minutes to prepare. What is important is that you establish a ritual that is kept weekly. In good times, Sunday nights will be fun. In bad times, Sunday nights will keep you together. You will come to look forward to these special dinners and so will your family. They will nurture your bodies, your marriage, and your family.

Here are two rules for our Sunday nights at the dinner table, which gives us an uninterrupted respectful hour together. One, no answering the telephone—cell, house, or business line—no text messaging, and no pagers. In fact, no electronic gadgets of any kind are allowed on, except for background music. Two, remember your table manners.

I am the cook in the family. I am interested in health and nutrition. I love family and friends gathering around the table, especially on Sunday nights. Sometimes I plan for days what I'm going to make, and some Sunday afternoons I happily begin cooking as early as 3:00 PM. Over the years, we've had hundreds of Sunday night dinners.

Sometimes we invite the kids' friends to join us. When they were young, we had lots of little girls over for macaroni and cheese. Then preteen adolescents sat moodily at our table with strange food diets—canned tomato soup made with water and forbidden ingredients such as, carbohydrates! Now, the teenage boyfriends come around hungry. Our Brugman Burgers are a hit with the boys. You'll want the boyfriends 'round at dinner to get to know them better, trust me.

We've also had our share of private meals with bursting teenage tears and ridiculous arguments on Sunday nights. Sometimes Glenn and I have had parental pep talks with each other before we call the kids in to sit down. "Okay, don't mention the Spanish test. Let's try and have fun. Crack some jokes, keep it light, and whatever you do, don't bring up their curfew. They will gang up on us, and I fear we'll give in. Let's talk about that after dinner."

Not every Sunday night dinner is perfect, but they are all wonderful in their own ways. They are a ritual our family enjoys, counts on, and will remember for life. It bonds us together.

Brugman Burgers

Delicious burgers begin with purchasing very lean ground beef. We like to buy locally raised, grain-fed, free-range beef. These purchase decisions support the sustainability of our environment and benefit our health, as well.

Prep time: 10 minutes
Cook time: 15 minutes
Serves: 4

1 pound lean ground beef
2 tablespoons Worcestershire sauce
2 tablespoons A1 Steak Sauce
1 tablespoon Montreal Steak Seasoning
½ cup chopped onion
2 tablespoons olive oil
2 tablespoons balsamic vinegar

Combine all ingredients in a large bow and mix well. Form thick patties. Grill or pan fry until the pink is almost gone. Serve with your favorite condiments, fixings, and Baked Garlic Fries.

Baked Garlic Fries (v)

6 russet potatoes slightly peeled (leave some skin on) and sliced into thick wedges
¼ cup olive oil
1 tablespoon sea salt
2 cloves garlic, crushed

Preheat your oven to 350°F.
Toss all ingredients in a large bowl. Bake at for 45 minutes on a baking sheet, turning the potatoes with a spatula twice. When golden brown and crispy on the outside, they are perfect.

Humor

Do you hear him chuckle often?

Marriages need large doses of laughter to thrive. In our materialistic society, adult lives have become riddled with stress and focused on getting ahead and getting "more" in order to become "happy." "Laughing all the way to the bank" is a common phrase. We pursue this end at a great expense—the loss of enjoying ourselves along the way.

Many lives lack fun and laughter on a regular basis. We have become accustomed to planning fun, but rarely do we allow it to happen spontaneously. Many of us postpone fun, laughter, and relaxation for so long that we have become not only unhappy, but we are also making ourselves sick. So many of us forget that life does not have to be so serious. What do you enjoy? What is your passion? What makes you laugh? You need to be a happy person in order to contribute to a happy marriage. Happy people laugh—a lot. Why not ask yourself what makes you happy and then ask your husband for support toward self-fulfillment? Should you reconsider your profession? I admire a woman who quit a job she disliked in corporate America and now runs a dog ranch on her property. She loves it. She has a deep boisterous laugh. I can tell that she is happy.

Is your husband fulfilled? Happy? Do you hear him chuckle often? How about roar with laughter? Laughter releases endorphins, which benefit our health immensely. Can you begin to see humor in stressful situations and change your reaction? Can you lighten up on the "old man"? Does all of the laundry really need to be folded before you go out? Does everything have to be scheduled? I suggest getting a few pets for lively entertainment and fun times. What movies make you laugh? Rent them. Enjoy the silly. Do something ridiculous today. Who is the funny one in your family? Let that person make you smile.

Glenn is gregarious—popular, everyone's friend, and funny. He knows exactly how to time a joke, having his audience hang on to every word as he draws them into his scene, pauses, and then delivers the punch line and has everyone cracking up. This amazes me. I have no idea how to accomplish this seemingly effortless manner of humor. He was crowned homecoming king in high school, of course. I'm grateful for his humor and easy manner, especially around the kids. He doesn't let life get too serious. And when a mishap occurs (as they seem to do with me quite often), he laughs about it—afterward.

Being happy-go-lucky is not something that comes easy for me. I'm quite the opposite of Glenn. I have an "A" type personality blessed with erratic social graces. I have to remind myself to have fun, relax, and laugh, even if it is at my own expense. I'm not very funny, and I can't tell a joke correctly either. But, I am amusing and definitely gullible. People laugh with me when I tell them my tales of unintentional, self-inflicted embarrassing mishaps. Glenn calls these minor mishaps pulling a "Wilson" (my maiden name). He says I could replace Lucy and star in a new TV show called, *I Love Wilson.*

He thoroughly enjoys laughing at and with me. He can't wait to say "Oh no" with a snicker when I tell him I pulled another "Wilson." He anticipates with delight my confessions, and I have to let him enjoy the moment for longer than I care to admit when he's laughing at me. I mean—*with* me. Some of my mishaps occur right before his very eyes, and much to his chagrin, he can't stop it from happening, like the mishap at the winery.

A few years ago I talked Glenn into buying a hundred-year-old beat up farmhouse on ten acres of land riddled with overgrown, thorny blackberry bushes. From a distance, you could envision the potential of the broken down barn, which sat awaiting capital. The good news is that the property was located in beautiful wine country in the Columbia River Gorge in Oregon. We slowly cultivated a naïve romantic notion of planting a vineyard on the land and decided to visit a local vintner, Bob Morris of Phelps Creek Vineyard, to begin our education.

We were anxious. We knew very little about wine and growing

grapes. Amazingly, we had been invited to his estate for a tour of his vineyard and into his home for a private wine tasting. As we pulled up the gravel drive and peered up at the massive decks overlooking the acres and acres of perfectly manicured vines, I began to prep Glenn, "Okay, we must buy some of Bob's wine," I said. "We cannot look cheap or appear as if we don't know what we are doing. We are beginning our reputation as professionals, wine connoisseurs, and future vintners in the same business as Bob." Glenn just nodded, silently, as he parked the car.

We tasted Bob's liquid gold chardonnay, his hypnotic Pinot Noir, his Private Reserve, and … well, I can't remember how many others because it was mid-day, and I was a little tipsy. I didn't know I had the option of not swallowing the wines we tasted. I thought it would be rude of me to not finish each glass poured because Bob had made the wines himself, and I didn't want to insult him.

"We will take a case of each," I blurted out after our last swallow. Bob gave me a long, big grin. Glenn stared at me. Bob's assistant wrote up our invoice to the tune of $1,200 for forty-eight bottles of wine. I had no idea what I was doing and obviously didn't calculate the math … 12 bottles at $15 and 12 bottles at $36 and 12 bottles at $20, etc. I swallowed hard. You can't imagine how embarrassed I was when I had to admit that I didn't realize I was spending that much. We ended up leaving with two cases and spent about $650, which was still three times our budget.

Eating my words was humbling, but we have had a good laugh over that one for years. I could have been mad at myself, but instead, I laughed at myself. Glenn could have been humiliated, upset, mad, fed up, or annoyed with me, but what did he do? He laughed and laughed right along with me all the way back to the farm house where I made him Herbed Chèvre Crostini drizzled with a Sweet Red Wine Reduction, while he uncased our new wine collection.

Delenee Brugman

Herbed Chèvre Crostini (v)

Prep time: 10 minutes
Cook time: 2 minutes
Serves: 4 to 6

One French baguette sliced diagonally about ¼ inch thick (12 slices)
Olive oil for brushing baguette slices
2 cups plain chèvre cheese (The French refer to fresh goat cheese as chèvre. Chèvre is the French word for goat.)
¼ cup fresh chopped dill
¼ cup fresh chopped chives

CHÈVRE
Cream together in separate bowls:

1 cup chèvre	1 cup chèvre
¼ cup fresh chopped dill	¼ cup fresh chopped chives

Preheat your oven to 350°F.
Brush the baguette slices lightly with olive oil and place them on a baking sheet. Toast them in the oven for about 2 minutes until golden, making a crostini.

When cool, add 1 tablespoon of the *dill* chèvre to six of the crostini. Add 1 tablespoon of the *chive* chèvre to the other six crostini, slightly smashing the cheese.

SWEET RED WINE REDUCTION
Prep time: 5 minutes
Cook time: 40 minutes
Serves: Makes about 2 cups and can be prepared in advance and kept un-refrigerated for two weeks.

2 cups sugar
4 cups red wine

1 tablespoon strawberry syrup (we like to use Torani)
1 tablespoon vanilla syrup (we like to use Torani)

In a medium saucepan, heat all the ingredients on medium/high heat and reduce until it is half of its original volume, stirring frequently. Use low heat for the last few minutes. It should resemble the consistency of syrup when finished.

PRESENTATION
Alternatively place dill and chive crostini on a serving plate and drizzle the dark, sweet, red wine reduction over them and onto the plate in creative swirls. Serve immediately or at room temperature. Wine pairing: Pinot Gris—a light crisp white wine that compliments the tartness of the chèvre.

ENDURE

Emotional and Physical Health
Care for yourself

Your marriage may suffer if you are not emotionally healthy. If you've got problems, delve into what's causing them and seek solutions. Many negative emotions originate from childhood. Lots of people grew up living within dysfunctional families. Divorce (and the resulting broken home), alcoholism, or verbal or physical abuse are prevalent problems today. Many of us have been damaged and hurt by one or several of these problems, experiencing the negative effects personally or through someone close that has not healed. Unfortunately, unless dealt with, the damage stays with us, and we continue to live in its repercussions long after the event has stopped. Often, it is passed on to loved ones (spouses and children) through a myriad of poor habits, continuing the damage cycle.

In those childhood dysfunctional and broken homes, we didn't see happy people or healthy relationships. We did not learn how to be happy ourselves, and we were not taught how to be happily married, either. A glaring indicator of this misery can be seen in our demand for antidepressants and the number of divorces filed each year. These numbers are rising, and I endeavor to lessen them.

The future of your emotional health is entirely up to you. Recognizing the problem(s) and having the resolve to change are the catalysts for growth. Read, my friend, read. Talk to professionals who are trained to guide you. Release your problems through writing, exercising, meditating or praying, joining group therapy, attending a retreat, or doing whatever it takes for you to transform. A metamorphosis is liberating.

Change the patterns and break the mold you were given. Refuse to repeat dysfunction. I did, and I found that by nurturing even the smallest change, further change came more easily. I also learned that emotional health is a practice. I practice allowing a healing strength move through me and out toward the world, remembering that I am bright, clear energy.

WAKE UP AND HUG

*W*ake up and hug to start your day with love. Wake up and hug to live a happier life. Wake up and hug, especially after a challenging night. Wake up and hug on a particularly beautiful day. Wake up and hug in front of your children. Wake up and hug while waiting for the coffee to brew, silent in each other's arms. Wake up and hug to reconnect, to feel your untouchable "we."

Every human adult needs several hugs a day for normal psychological well-being and children need even more. Nothing else in this world feels as good as Glenn's arms around me with my head resting on his chest, if only for a moment. If he adds a long, strong squeeze at the end, I'm awash with love, protection, safety, and comfort, and the whole world melts away. Hugging Glenn is a meditation of joy.

PHYSICAL HEALTH AND STRESS LEVELS

*Y*our marriage may be compromised if you are not physically healthy. Living with vigor and having a sense of well being brings vitality to your marriage. Be as physically healthy as you can at every age and don't take on more than you can handle. Keep your stress levels in check. Too much stress negatively affects our health.

A safety procedure that flight attendants recommend on airplanes reminds me to breathe. "Put on your oxygen mask first and then assist others." Often, women, who tend to be the primary caretakers of the family, are so consumed with assisting others, including their husbands, that they literally run out of air. But, amazingly, caring for you first gives you more energy to care for others.

But this is not why you should do it. Care for yourself because you love yourself. No one else is able to meet your needs as well as you. You know when you need rest, exercise, nutrition, excitement, adventure, or time away. Your husband can't be everything for you or force you take care of yourself. That responsibility is yours.

When you are well cared for by you, you become balanced, calm, and able to handle anything life brings with grace.

SEPARATE, BUT OVERLAPPING VACATIONS

*Y*ou might want to consider a retreat away from your husband and your family by taking a separate, but overlapping, vacation.

Separate but overlapping vacations, even if one of you is at home, that end together at a special meeting place renews both of you. Marriages need breaks. Each partner needs a good chunk of time without their spouse to be with his or her own thoughts, to de-stress, and to have some fun. Meet your hubby on day seven, happily relaxed, for a couple more days of vacation just with him.

Glenn and I have had separate and overlapping vacations, and they are definitely healthy for our relationship. The time away allows for introspection and appreciation. Looking forward to seeing your man and longing for him is a great aphrodisiac to your reunion.

When you get home from vacation, try and stay in the carefree mood. Once I'm back home, hitting the ground running tends to be my modus operandi. I have to remind myself to slow down or upon waking my mind starts repeating the same old lines. Where is my cell phone? What time is it? How much time do I have until I need to do XYZ? What does Glenn need? What do the kids need? It goes on and on and on. Then I feed the dogs, let the cats out, turn on the computer, and before I know it, the morning is gone, and the relaxation from the vacation is only a distant memory.

So instead, I try to be present upon waking and listen to my inner guidance. I offer myself a few minutes of silence. With a long, relaxed exhaling breath, I have trained myself to think, *what can I do for myself today?* Then that relaxed feeling resurfaces. The balance begins to emerge. This morning I thought, *I have enough time for a bath. I will exercise by noon, and for lunch I will make myself curried chicken salad lettuce wraps. Now, that feels like a spa day!*

Curried Chicken Salad Lettuce Wraps

*Think of the lettuce in this recipe as a tortilla. While making the wrap,
you might long for that big crusty baguette slathered in mayo, but if you
are watching your girlish figure, a lettuce wrap is a delicious alternative.
Once you bite into it, you won't miss the bread. The ingredients are
nourishing and satisfying.*

Prep time: 10 minutes
Cook time: None
Serves: 4 to 6

5 boneless, skinless pre-cooked chicken breasts, cut into strips
½ cup low-fat mayonnaise
2 tablespoons yellow curry powder
1 green (or tart) apple, cored and chopped
A handful of raisins
A whole scallion, chopped
½ cup store-bought ginger-mango chutney
1 handful of sliced cashews
1 handful of chopped fresh cilantro
Salt
Freshly ground black pepper
Romaine lettuce leaves

In a medium-sized mixing bowl, fold together all of the ingredients,
except the lettuce. Spoon about a cup down the middle of a lettuce leaf
and wrap around. If using romaine, cut out the bottom "white" center
core. Warm up some of the ginger-mango chutney to use as a perfect
dipping sauce.

Other filling suggestions: Tuna salad with capers and red onion; steak
slices with marinated roasted red peppers; hamburger patties (formed
in long rectangles) and low-fat condiments; sautéed teriyaki tofu and
a jubilee of fresh stir-fried veggies (zucchini strips, carrot strips, bean
sprouts, cabbage, and cilantro); chicken with pesto and fresh basil.

PRESENTATION

Cut lettuce wrap on an angle and stack crosswise on a plate with your dipping sauce in a small cup on the side.

$\mathcal{F}$riends and Family

Lessons to learn

MARRIED FRIENDS AND FAMILY

$\mathcal{I}$ encourage you to spend time with other married couples. Ask them their recipe for love. Listen. You can learn a great deal, especially if they have a good marriage. I ask the wives how they've done it, how they've stayed married. I get many different responses, all of which I've taken to heart, and I have appreciated the candidness of their answers.

You can also learn what to do and what not to do simply by watching and by listening to other couples' interactions. Notice how they talk to each other. Notice how they don't. Notice how they talk about each other. You and your hubby can chat later about what you think works and what you think doesn't. Emulate the good.

A few words of caution: Parents, please don't just get together with other parents and talk about your kids all night long, or worse, get all of you together (parents and kids) and watch them toddle across the floor. Spend some time with other married couples in an adult environment. Hire a sitter to stay upstairs with the kids while you throw a dinner party downstairs if you must.

If you find yourselves in the company of a dysfunctional couple, don't get swept up into their dilemmas. They have negative dramatic scenarios you won't want to be involved in. It could strain your own relationship, especially if the women see eye to eye, and the husbands side together. Perhaps seeing each of them separately as friends is best.

I encourage you to create a marriage that becomes one of the tried and true relationships other couples look up to. I hope they will ask you, "What is your secret? How do you two stay together?"

DIVORCED FRIENDS AND FAMILY

*S*ome of my greatest teachers on marriage are my divorced friends and family. I've learned, of course, what not to do through them, but more importantly, I take it as a reminder to work harder on my own marriage.

Many divorced couples we know, including both the husbands and the wives, have later separately confessed, "If only I knew then what I know now, I would have never divorced. I would have tried harder." This always amazes us, because we watched and listened endlessly to their excruciating separations and divorces. The unattractive title "divorced" follows their names like a stain. Loss, pain, grief, disappointment, and regret are negative emotions they own. They are easy to recognize. Swimming in the dating pool again is what they now endure.

Just this week I met two different women who recently divorced after twenty years. Their stories sadden me. They had beaten the odds and had triumphed through great challenges, raised children, and spent two decades together, yet still chose to suffer one of life's most devastating and most stressful events: divorce. The emotional trauma their families experienced was and is devastating, especially for their children.

The blame, the rationalization, and the justification of their divorce are a familiar story. "He was too this or not enough of that." "He didn't allow me to be me; I felt controlled." "I compromised myself with him." "We didn't work on the marriage very much during parenting, and after the kids left home, there wasn't anything there." "My husband was an alcoholic." "He cheated. He lied." "Can't you see why we divorced?"

These may be seriously significant reasons to consider divorce, but I'd like to give you some encouragement to envision working through problems toward a positive solution rather than solve it with a negative one.

However, if you are experiencing any kind of physical or mental abuse, your first step is to immediately seek professional help and ensure the safety of yourself and your children. Then you can work on healing the relationship, if possible.

Tolerating dysfunction is so unhealthy. If your husband has serious problems that directly affect you, think about this: These are your problems, too. Don't be codependent during your marriage, give up, divorce, and then cast the blame on your ex-spouse. Endurance, guts, and compromise (or as I call it: co-marriage-promise) are essential characteristics of a strong marriage.

And, remember, it's not too late. Whether you are in year one or year fifty, it is not too late to heal your marriage.

If you have said the "D" word a thousand times to each other, your marriage can still be healed. If there has been the ultimate betrayal of adultery, your marriage can still be healed. Everything is forgivable. I'm not saying forgettable or that enduring and healing these situations will be easy. What I'm saying is that they can be endured, and they can be healed.

If you are separated now, and one of you packed your bags and is living with another person, it still might not be too late to heal your marriage. Oftentimes, the one who leaves is the one who wants to come back at some point in the future, full of sorrow and regret. After finding out that the grass isn't greener on the other side of the fence, they want to come home and water their own lawn. Much pain and anguish will now be part of your history together. Professional counsel is advisable.

It is my opinion that there are a significant number of divorces that need not occur. And, those divorces lead to more divorces. A first marriage has the greatest chance of success. The success rate of a subsequent marriage decreases. Imagine, it could actually be harder the next time around.

A DIVORCÉE STORY

A multiple divorcée shared her story with me. She uses the alphabet as a metaphor for marriage. Here's how it goes: You start out with your first husband, and you go through ABC, the honeymoon phase, and on to DEFGHI, where problems arise and endurance and acceptance are required. By JKL, you are ready for someone "better" or "different." You aren't willing to work hard enough to get past the middle of the alphabet with that person. You fantasize about someone more suited to you who doesn't have these problems and believe that it could be easier, and that you will know better next time. You'd rather start over, and you do. There is your first divorce.

You remarry. The problem is that you don't realize that with husband number two, you eventually arrive at the middle of the alphabet again, and this relationship has other problems you didn't expect. You succumb to the truth: you are unwilling to do the hard work of that relationship, and, of course, it is much easier to divorce the second time when you are ready for someone "better" or "different."

You start regretting your first divorce and begin to think that husband number one wasn't so bad after all. You say to yourself, *why didn't I just work harder on my first marriage?* Too bad he's also remarried. So, after awhile, you divorce again and go searching for husband number three. You say to yourself, unconvincingly, *this time, I know exactly what I want and what I don't want, and this marriage is sure to work out.* Gradually, nine years have gone by, and you're contemplating divorce number three.

If you, dear reader, are contemplating divorce, please take the entire afternoon to quietly and patiently contemplate how you can heal your marriage, perhaps with the help of my words and my stories, while making my most treasured recipe, Baked Apple and Butternut Squash Soup. It will fill your home with sweet and savory aromas, nourish your body, and soothe your aching, wounded heart.

Baked Apple and Butternut Squash Soup (v)

Prep time: 1 hour
Bake time: 1 hour
Serves: 8 to 10 (You'll want leftovers and it freezes well.)

3 medium butternut squash—4 pounds total
3 Fuji apples
3 cups apple juice
4 cups chicken stock (or vegetable stock)
2 cups chopped sweet onion
6 tablespoons butter
2 tablespoons yellow curry powder
Salt
Freshly ground pepper

Preheat your oven to 350°F.
Chop the squash in thirds and remove the seeds. Salt and pepper it and bake for 1 hour. Peel, core, and chop the apples in half and bake in the apple juice for 30 minutes.

Meanwhile, chop up a very large sweet onion and sauté it on low heat in a large pot with the butter and curry powder. Cover it and cook for 30 minutes, stirring occasionally.

When the apples (save the apple juice) and squash are baked, take them out of the oven to cool. When you can touch the squash, scoop out the squash meat, discard the skins, and add the squash, baked apples, and stock to the pot of sautéed onions. Puree until smooth with your magic wand. (You could use a blender, but it can be messy.) Then, fold in the apple juice.

PRESENTATION
When serving guests, I like to share with them how healthy this soup is. No heavy creams are added—it is simply baked apples, butternut

squash, and curried onions pureed with stock and apple juice. I've served this soup out of fine china bowls on Thanksgiving Day, in big coffee mugs at the kitchen table, in camping thermoses when on a hike, and in dainty little appetizer cups at dinner parties. For all occasions, people like to dip bread into the soup, so be sure to have a fresh baked loaf on hand.

Progress

It shall unfold

One of my favorite phrases is "It shall unfold." If you are giving love, time, and good energy to your marriage, you can expect positive progress and the rewards of an unfolding love story.

There will be times when your marriage feels like it's regressing, but even during difficult transitions, there is an opportunity for progress, which is growth. Don't be fooled: you will never "arrive." It doesn't exist! Don't cheat yourself by waiting for your marriage to be perfect. Don't say to yourself, *if we could just do this or when he does that, then we will be happily married.* Don't postpone happiness. You can choose to be happily married now.

Life is complicated, fleeting, incredibly challenging, and evolving by the minute. Be at ease with the journey and celebrate your little happy progressive steps, which are the flame kindlers to the fire of your love.

Today, acknowledge him for something … anything. Glenn was very patient with me when I clogged the kitchen sink, and he had to undo the pipes below to remove the now solidified candle wax I poured down the drain when cleaning candleholders with hot water. This was my latest "Wilson." By the way, when he came back from buying a drain snake at the hardware store, he was greeted to a kitchen full of smoke as I had absentmindedly left the dirty omelet pan on low and went to walk the dogs … ooops. His patience and my acknowledgement equal progress. This is moving in the right direction.

Did you apologize for yesterday's slip of the tongue? If yes, then progress. Don't beat yourself up because you snapped, again.

Congratulate yourself for becoming more aware that you wish to change. Congratulate yourself for being humble enough to apologize. Pat yourself on the forehead and say aloud, "progress, not perfection." Think, *I am working on me; I am working on we.*

Many wives are going through similar emotions and trials within their marriages. I want you to know that it's okay. Just keep at it. I gave my rough manuscript of this book to a long-time friend who has also been married for more than twenty years. I wanted her opinion. Her husband and Glenn are good friends, and they remain our nearest and dearest married couple. We have been friends with them through our entire marriage. As we were sitting in the back seat of the car while our husbands drove us to breakfast, I handed her the book. She read my introduction and instantly began to cry. Really, unstoppable tears just kept streaming down her face.

Our husbands, who were in the front seats of the car, kept glancing back at us wondering what in the world was going on. After all, it was 9:30 in the morning. Their young daughter kept asking, "What's wrong, Mom?" Nothing was wrong. It was just that she knew—she is one of the women who has flirted, communicated, loved, endured, and given her life's energy to her marriage. And she knows how much goes into it and what it means to be married this long and to have progressed this far.

At breakfast, we drank lattes and chai teas with soy milk, sitting outside in the sunshine at a café on a southeast Portland street corner, enjoying a simple meal with good friends—one of life's greatest pleasures. We had big appetites that morning and ordered huge plates of pancakes, sausages, eggs, and cottage fries.

By late that afternoon, back at our house, we were getting a little bit hungry, again. I wanted to make my friends something warm and sweet, just the way I feel about them. So, I decided to make them the delightful appetizer I call Sweet Honey Brie. I drizzled a whole Brie with honey and sprinkled it with sliced almonds and baked it just until soft. Then I poured a basket of fresh, ripe, soft, fuchsia-colored raspberries over the top before I served it. They cooed with delight.

Sweet Honey Brie (v)

In France, they might serve this for dessert.

Prep time: 5 minutes
Cook time: 5 minutes
Serves: 2 to 4

A triangular wedge of French Brie
A tablespoon of honey
A handful of sliced almonds
Fresh fruit (berries or granny smith apple slices)
A baguette or water crackers

Preheat your oven to 350°F.
Place your wedge of Brie in the center of an oven-safe dish. Drizzle it with the honey and sprinkle the sliced almonds on top of the Brie and all around the dish. Warm it until the center is soft and just starting to melt—about 5 minutes. Watch it closely because the Brie can quickly melt into an oil-like substance, which you don't want. Slightly melted and still soft is the desired result.

PRESENTATION
Place the hot dish on top of a larger, cool dish or platter and garnish with fresh fruit and baguette slices or crackers. Serve it with an interesting knife because you are an interesting wife.

This appetizer is a real crowd pleaser. If hosting or taking it to a party, use a whole Brie wheel and triple the other ingredients.

Money and Abundance

Unexpected blessings

Over the course of a long marriage personal economic changes are bound to occur. How you allow them to affect your marriage is how you will either weaken or strengthen it. Problems with money can challenge a marriage when the partners allow the stress and struggle of making and keeping money strain their relationship. Dissolving a marriage over money is ridiculous. Money is nothing more and nothing less a medium of exchange. It represents energy. Harnessing that energy so that it flows toward your bank account is defined as uniquely as the individuals who share the account and their ability to create opportunities in myriad of ever changing circumstances.

During your marriage you will probably experience both times of abundance and times of lack. They do not appear in any particular order and even when you think you've got it all planned out and have "made it" things can change. Key to understanding your relationship with money and how it affects your marriage is keeping your eye on the abundance that you do have, no matter what the checkbook reads.

In our marriage we have experienced times of great wealth (European vacations for us and our children, private high school tuitions, a life in Hawaii) and great hardship (literally there have been two distinct years, once early in our marriage and once recently, where we have been down to $200 in our bank account with no income in sight).

During times of wealth the living is easy and gratitude ought to be a daily thought. During times of lack the living is harder and real gratitude for any abundance brought your way is paramount. See your marriage as part of the abundance you have.

You can get through tough financial times together. I've been there. Hold hands and bravely hold onto your marriage. When you've weathered the storm together and are sailing on calmer seas your marriage and love will be deeply strengthened.

The spring of 1991 gave us a renewed faith in the magic of the universe and the unexpected blessings that come to support and carry you along.

We purchased a 1940s two-bedroom fixer-upper house the year we were pregnant with our second child. We found a savvy real estate broker and a swanky loan officer who worked together to pull off the deal, and my mother loaned us the money for the down payment with a second mortgage placed on the house. We really couldn't afford either of the mortgages, but we took a leap of faith. I was passionate about nesting, and I simply had to raise our family in our own home. It can be a scary prospect to disappoint a pregnant woman, so Glenn went right along with me and signed those daunting loan documents. And there we were, living the American dream—two kids and a house mortgaged to the hilt.

By the time our baby was born, we were maxed-out financially. Glenn was working full time, but the income never seemed enough with two growing children and two mortgages. We didn't want to leave our children at day care and send me off to work, so we chose to forego my ability to earn an outside income. We were determined to give our children the time it requires to mother them, which they needed and deserved. This is a choice we never regretted, and we are most proud of this conviction. There were, however, months where we did not know how we would put food on the table and pay all the bills.

Out of both desperation and resourcefulness, that spring we decided to plant a vegetable garden in anticipation that by summer we could literally eat the fruits of our labor. Early one Sunday morning the kids and I sat on an old cement cinder block at the back of the yard and patiently watched Glenn dig deep into mother earth, tilling her soil. We eagerly waited for him to tell us when we could plant a little seed of hope into the ground.

Our morning magically and dramatically changed. Suddenly we

heard an unexpected sound. Clink, clink, clink. Glenn's shovel hit something metal and hundreds of coins burst out, spilling onto the barren soil. As he slowly turned his shovel, we gazed upon a compost of coins, and then he dug up an interesting metal box. He brushed the dirt off with his bare hands and pried open the lid. It was full of gray plastic film containers and prescription drug containers. We wondered, *have we found buried drugs?*

Glenn picked up one of the prescription drug containers and held it up to the sun. We saw a stack of silver dollar coins encapsulated in the yellowish plastic. The next one sheltered a fat roll of green paper bills with the number fifty on the outside bill. That color of green was greener than any plant I was hoping to raise. Glenn and I stared at each other for a moment, in disbelief, and then with the excitement of children on Christmas morning, we ran to the house with Glenn carrying the box and a baby bouncing on my hip.

We laid out newspapers and dropped the dirty, rusty metal box on the kitchen table. Our three-year-old daughter who, of course, believed in fairy tales, happily skipped around our kitchen table sweetly singing, "We found a buried treasure! We found a buried treasure!" while Glenn reopened the lid.

It was a surreal experience. The total treasure came to more than $4,000 in cash. Glenn had an instant coin collection. That afternoon, after the excitement had worn off and thankfulness took its place, I took a curly fifty-dollar bill that wouldn't lie flat and drove to the grocery store in a daze of utter amazement. I realized again, as I have been shown before, that the universe provides, and with a little faith, you will be sustained along the right path.

I arrived home with the fixings for a Sunday night feast of Garlic Roasted Chicken and Sea-Salted Vegetables. That evening began our coveted tradition of family Sunday night dinners, which was created out of thankfulness, honoring our good fortune. I humbly baked and cooked quietly listening to Glenn while he sat at our kitchen table with his new coin collection, stacking them in piles according to their dates, telling me about each one, relishing in our discovery.

The buried treasure was a precious gift to us, and we treated it with due respect. We carefully used its wealth slowly, and only when absolutely necessary did we open the box. By stretching the money along a path of determination, I was able to stay home with my children full time until they enrolled in preschool and kindergarten. I gave them not only quality, but also an abundance of time while I nursed and fed them, and watched them grow right before my very eyes.

Garlic Roasted Chicken and Sea-Salted Vegetables (v)

Prep time: 10 minutes
Bake time: Vegetables 30 minutes; chicken 1¼ hours
Serves: 4 to 6

A whole chicken, skin on and bones in
7 cloves garlic, whole and peeled for stuffing the bird
Sea salt
Freshly ground pepper
Olive oil
A variety of vegetables to roast—vary texture and color
Suggestions: Potatoes (red, Russet, Yukon Gold, fingerling); carrots; yams; sweet potatoes; broccoli; tomatoes; cauliflower; brussels sprouts; yellow and red onions; green, yellow and red peppers; squash (butternut, pumpkin, acorn, zucchini, yellow)

Preheat your oven to 350°F.
Get out two medium-sized roasting pans. One is for the chicken, and the other is for the vegetables. Chop the hard vegetables ½ inch thick and chop the softer vegetables 1 inch thick, so that the baking time is about even. Stuff the inside of the bird with the garlic. Baste the chicken and vegetables with olive oil and sprinkle with sea salt and freshly ground pepper. Bake uncovered.

Remove the vegetables at 30 minutes and serve them at room temperature when the chicken is finished baking. Roast the chicken an additional 30 to 45 minutes (depending on the size). Usually, when the juices run clear and the legs are very loose, it is fully cooked. Let it rest 10 minutes before carving, allowing the juices to soak in.

PRESENTATION

The wafts of garlic, onions, and sweet potatoes will be heady. You'll be so pleased with yourself in making a simple and savory meal that you'll want to light a few candles on the table and relax into its enjoyment. I like serving this gorgeous bird on a bed of rosemary sprigs from the garden on a large platter with the room temperature roasted vegetables surrounding it.

$\mathscr{R}$ealignment
Surviving tough times

$\mathscr{S}$ome years you may experience enormous amounts of stress and great change. Glenn and I are proof that a marriage can survive through tough times with a little bit of grace and a lot of resilience. We have lived through many challenges. Here are a few of them:

Surprise, we're pregnant! A beloved parent passes. You're fired! (Uh—that one happened to me.) Unemployment. Illness. Relocation. Four-and-a-half years of monthly orthodontic bills for two smiling girls. Refinancing the house—again. What else? The family dog died. Didn't get that promotion we were counting on.

Want more? The roof of our fixer-upper home leaked all across the center beam, and we didn't have enough buckets, pots, pans, or towels to mop up the tropical storm pouring in. Our eldest teen dislocated her shoulder six times and needed surgery. We were threatened with a lawsuit and the guy wanted $100,000. Our youngest teen wants a BlackBerry, a flat-screen TV, and $200 designer jeans. Our COBRA insurance benefits ran out at the same time our savings account did. We started a new business during the unexpected worldwide economic recession.

Shall I continue? Menopause. Manopause. (Yes, it exists.) Midlife crisis. An auto accident totaled the car. Handfuls of financial investments turned into fiascos. College tuition, room, and board now due. What else? Denied life insurance. Aging. Credit cards. Empty nest. More aging! You get the picture. Life happens!

When we are in the eye of a storm, I think about that little poem I heard on my wedding day ... in sickness and in health, for richer or for poorer ... until death do us part. Humph, it must be a true story.

These kinds of stressful experiences test our marriage rigorously. When we make it through them, we have greater strength as individuals and as a married couple. We've learned not to walk down the miserable hall of regret. It doesn't serve any purpose. We were cautioned by a wise elder not to blame ourselves or each other for taking risks or making decisions that turned out differently than we planned. These lessons have great value in them and can only be learned through overcoming challenges.

Glenn and I call these times realignment periods. It is a difficult phrase to swallow. Sometimes it feels like the sting of citrus on our parched lips, but we both know that we will make it through with resilience and try to gracefully bear it. He's better at handling it than I am, but I know it won't break us. Life has many transitions. Accept them when they arise. Change is really the only thing we can count on as a constant.

When you're faced with challenges, I recommend making a large, warm bowl of comfort food. For us, it's Roasted Pepper Marinara. Boil some pasta and smother it with the sauce. After dinner, take time for hugging and healing and then brainstorm a plan—recreating your life. Knowing that these trying times will surely come helps you accept them. Denial or avoidance will only increase the intensity of any dilemma you face. If you are reading this early in your marriage, please discuss action plans and "what if" scenarios so that you are semi-prepared. So many people think, "That won't happen to me, to us." But, as I've learned, no one is invincible.

Roasted Pepper Marinara (v)

A large, warm bowl of comfort food

Prep time: 30 minutes
Cook time: 20 minutes
Serves: 4 to 6

2 red peppers
2 yellow peppers
2 green peppers
1 large chopped yellow onion
2 large chopped tomatoes
¼ cup olive oil
1 cup chicken stock
1 cup heavy cream
A handful of chopped fresh basil
1 teaspoon fresh rosemary
1 teaspoon fresh oregano
Salt
Freshly ground pepper

Preheat your oven to broil.
Broil the peppers whole, turning once, blackening the skins. Let them cool to the touch and then scrape off half of the blackened skin. (Leaving on some of the charred pieces gives the marinara a smoky flavor.) Remove the seeds and chop the flesh. Put the peppers, onion, and tomatoes into a large skillet with the olive oil and sauté uncovered on low for 30 minutes, stirring frequently, until the onions are tender and translucent. Puree until smooth with your magic wand. Add all of the other ingredients and heat through.

PRESENTATION

We love this marinara on top of meats or pastas and as a dipping sauce for focaccia. Sometimes we add more cream and turn it into a soup.

117

$\mathscr{O}$pportunity and Support

Tell him "You can."

OPPORTUNITY

$\mathscr{G}$ive your husband the opportunity to try any and every passion he's interested in. In fact, be a foundation of loving openness and help him fulfill his dreams. Give him the encouragement to feel safe in expressing his "I've always wanted to." Help him find the path and get involved. Does he need a nudge or perhaps a push off the cliff? Whatever it is, you will know. Trust your intuition. Summon the courage required to stand behind him, becoming the best wife you can be. Don't be afraid and don't be the one to hold your man back.

My heart breaks to hear older people wistfully looking back on their lives and complaining about settling for less, sorrowfully singing their would've, could've, and should've songs. I feel compassion for those people who think that a wonderful, fulfilled, creative life is not for them and is reserved only for the smart, the rich, the movie stars, the educated, or other people.

Who told your husband, "You can't"? Perhaps it was a parent, a teacher, a minister, a friend, or an ex. Dear wife, don't let it be you. Tell him "You can." Tell him "Yes, you can take that opportunity, and I will be by your side."

Here are the times when I've mustered up the courage and said to my husband with gusto, "Go for it."

The yoga school in San Francisco

Moving to Oahu, Hawaii
The four years of night school for his MBA
The video production company
Quitting his corporate job and leaving a secure salary and benefits
Café Reese

To bring you up to date, just last month, on our twenty-first wedding anniversary, we asked each other the question: What would you do with the rest of your life if money was no object, and you were in good health? His reply, "I would travel throughout Italy playing the guitar." I'll keep you posted.

SUPPORT

After you give him the "Go for it," back him up with your support. When you offer unconditional love and support to your best friend, lover, and spouse, then that individual has the security and the room to flourish or fail without consequences. Who else believes in your man more than you? It is amazing what one can accomplish with the security of acceptance, regardless of the outcome. Believe in your spouse and watch him grow.

When Glenn decided to go back to college (at age forty) and finish his bachelor's degree, the timing was, ah, rather challenging. We were both working full time management jobs (me commuting two hours a day, roundtrip, to work), and our girls were still in grade school. Nonetheless, I took on more than my share. I was happy to help him achieve this goal. I thought his degree would set a good example for the kids, as we wanted them to go to college.

Glenn's pursuit of his bachelor's degree lasted two long years, during which time he attended night school, studied, wrote papers, and did school projects on the weekends with his study group (with whom I think he spent more time with than us). We didn't see him much as he, too, worked his full-time job during the day. I became the backbone of the family, giving my full support to each of my household students.

It was worth it. We were so proud of him at his graduation ceremony. He had obtained a Bachelor of Arts Degree in Business. Then, much to my surprise, the following night (just after my relief), he told me that he wanted to attend another two years of night school in pursuit of his master's degree. Believe me, I was not thrilled. I actually (much to my regret and chagrin) said no. Yet, in time, I did agree. How could I not continue to support the man I love in furthering his education?

Two years later, at Glenn's MBA graduation party in our home, before we served Coconut Cream Mahi Mahi over jasmine rice to our guests who had traveled across the Pacific Ocean to celebrate with us, Glenn surprised me by standing up and giving me a toast thanking me for my love, patience, and support. He told everyone he couldn't have done it without me and then presented me with a ring box that held three thin bands carved like bamboo and bonded together.

He said to me, "The copper band represents the past; the gold band represents the present; and the platinum band represents our future together." The guests were teary-eyed and then burst into applause. I was touched, and I still am. I wear these rings around my neck on a long, braided gold chain. During those four years of support, you bet I made a lot of meals. I would set plates of food on his desk and leave the room, quietly closing the door behind me.

Coconut Cream Mahi Mahi

The delicate scent of jasmine flowers is released during the cooking of the jasmine rice. And the aromas of simmering coconut milk, lime juice, and lemon grass will entice you to put on a sarong and eat this dish barefoot in the garden lit with tiki torches.

Prep time: 10 minutes
Cook time: 30 minutes
Serves: 4

2 cups fish stock
4 cups unsweetened coconut milk
2 tablespoons fish sauce
2 tablespoons sugar
4 tablespoons freshly squeezed lime juice
1 stalk lemon grass
Salt
Freshly ground pepper
¼ cup olive oil (to pan-fry the fish)
4 6-ounce servings of Mahi Mahi fish fillets
A handful of cilantro leaves for edible garnish
2 cups jasmine rice

Follow the package directions and make the jasmine rice. In a deep saucepan, add the fish stock, coconut milk, fish sauce, sugar, lime juice, and lemon grass. Simmer on medium heat for 30 minutes, stirring frequently and reducing it in half, until it becomes a cream sauce.

Meanwhile, salt and pepper the fish and pan-fry it in a little olive oil to brown it on both sides and cook it until the center has just turned white. Be careful not to overcook, as fish continues to cook after it is removed from the heat.

PRESENTATION

Place a large scoop of jasmine rice in the center of each plate. Pour ¼ cup of the coconut cream sauce on the rice. Top with a fish fillet and another ½ cup of the coconut cream sauce on the fish. Garnish with cilantro leaves.

$\mathscr{S}$pace and a Place of His Own
Reading his signals

SPACE

$\mathscr{I}$ am prone, like many women, to continuous, seemingly endless female chatter. I've still got work to do on this one. But, I have learned to recognize Glenn's signals that he needs some space, and I give it to him.

When he's reading the paper, I won't interrupt. If he's watching sports on TV, I leave him be. If he's meticulously polishing the car, I know he needs time alone. His signals are usually subtle. He starts doing something without saying much. The tricky part is my recognizing his need for this space. He doesn't usually ask for it, and sometimes it seems as if he's ignoring me. But, I remind myself that he just needs time away from me. He needs time to process life and think quietly by focusing on one simple task. He needs time to forget the demanding responsibilities of life and the pressure of its relentless cycle.

Doing a focused activity, especially if it requires his undivided attention, can refresh a man. It doesn't mean he is not concerned with you or the latest issue in your lives, it just means he's processing it in his own way. Resolutions to problems often come to a man after time off. Women need to talk things out to process them. Men focus on a task and process.

If you bug him for attention when you're getting the signals that he needs some space, he may tune you out by half listening, leaving you both frustrated. It is best to give him some space (yes, it could mean hours) and reserve your exasperations and needs until later. They may simmer down and not be so overwhelming after awhile.

A PLACE OF HIS OWN

*M*en need a place of their own to go to when they need some space. My inspiration to give Glenn a place of his own, in every home we have lived in, came from a house featured in a magazine. A wife, who is an interior designer, created a study for her husband and decorated it with rich and earthy materials, worn leather couches, deer horn lamps, found antiques, and piles of books. There was a lair-like quality to it, and it had a fireplace, but the best part was that the windows overlooked the sea. I've stared at that magazine layout many times. I was inspired. I imagined a man could regain his thoughts, plan his future, and accomplish much in such a wonderful, decadent place.

Unfortunately, most of us don't live in large houses featured in magazines overlooking the sea. Perhaps, your man's solitary space will have to be in a hall closet for now. Look around your home. Where could you create a place just for him? Can you give up the rarely used dining room and drape it off for his new passion? Is there a bit of square footage under the stairs? Could you build something in the backyard? What about the garage? Is there a guest cottage? Could you enclose the patio? How often do you use the back porch? Would your basement be conducive to soundproofing for his drum set? Is there a rooftop? Could you see it used in a different manner? What about the guest room? Do you think you could give up your walk-in closet? (Of course, I'm just kidding.)

What this room becomes depends on your man and your home. Is he an intellectual? Give him a study. Does he like to ponder the meaning of life? Give him a drawing room. Has he a passion for oil painting? Give him an art studio. Is he an athlete? Give him a gym. Is he a do-it-yourself man? Give him a tool shop. Does he want to pursue his musical interests? Give him a music room. Does he cherish books? Give him a library. Is he a movie buff? Give him a home theater. Does he like to watch sports with his buddies? Give him a sports bar. Does he want to create his own business? Give him the place to do so. And, by the way, once you've given him this place, celebrate and make love in it. He will have the nicest memory of you while working in there.

The first place Glenn had was an old garage full of ironworker's tools left over from the previous owner of our fixer-upper house. It had lots of metal parts and iron cranks, whose purpose we could never quite figure out. The garage windows didn't overlook the sea but, rather, a dirt patch in our back yard. I thought it had great potential.

It had a solid wood workshop counter, and it had a door you could lock, plus a sink. Well, frankly, it smelled and looked manly. Glenn spent hours out there, tinkering … puttering … fixing things … I don't know, whatever he wanted to do. He usually popped open a beer and went inside late in the afternoons on the weekends. His father had such a place, too, and Glenn remembers hanging out with his dad in the garage. I left him alone when he was in there. We parked the cars in the carport instead of the garage, so he could have this place. I'd call him to dinner later. He seemed relaxed when he left it and rejoined us.

In our home now, the living room has grown into Glenn's music room. His forty-something buddies show up every Tuesday night for their all "boy" band practice. They bring over their keyboards and their electric guitars, and they leave their 100-watt Marshall amps behind. I drew a three-foot high treble cleft insignia on the wall behind the piano, christening the music room. Glenn's guitars are strewn about the room, and he casually picks them up and strums, while I cook dinner. I don't mind sharing the living room with Glenn and his band members because I see how much he enjoys it. Sometimes I make the band members a treat, like warm, bubbling ramekins of Blueberry-Blackberry Cobbler. But before I leave the house the house every Tuesday night, I make sure to warn the neighbors.

Blueberry-Blackberry Cobbler (v)

*This will draw him out toward the kitchen
in search of vanilla ice cream.*

Prep time: 10 minutes
Cook time: 20 minutes
Serves: 2

FRUIT BOTTOM
1 cup fresh blueberries
1 cup fresh blackberries
1 teaspoon sugar
1 tablespoon honey
1 tablespoon flour
1 teaspoon freshly squeezed lemon juice

TOPPING
1 cup of granola cereal (no nuts or dried fruits)
2 tablespoons cold butter, cut into little pieces
A pinch of salt
A pinch of cinnamon
A pinch of nutmeg
A pinch of sugar for the top, just before you pop it in the oven

Preheat your oven to 375°F.
In a medium-sized bowl combine the ingredients for the fruit bottom
and set aside.

Meanwhile, butter the bottom of a small tart dish or two ramekins.
In a separate bowl, add the topping ingredients and stir with a fork
making little buttery granola crumbles. Spoon your fruit mixture into
the bottom of the buttered tart dish (or ramekins) and top with the
granola mixture and a pinch of sugar. Bake 20 minutes, until the berry
juice is bubbling.

Delenee Brugman

PRESENTATION
You've got to let this cool down before serving. Serve with whipped cream or a scoop of vanilla ice cream for dessert, or with yogurt for breakfast.

Boys' Night Out
Girl's night in

Glenn gets together with his buddies often, and I encourage it. He plays poker, goes to sports bars, and has weekly band practice with the guys. On some Saturdays, he rides his bike with a father-son team and is gone half the day. Boys' night out also has turned into boys' weekend with overnight trips of happy men hiking, biking, rafting, drinking, eating, and playing paint ball.

He does not have to ask permission to go out, and I don't imply that he does. I don't call him to see when he's coming home. I don't make him feel guilty, and I don't control when, where, or why. I trust him and allow him this basic masculine need to macho-up with his buddies and, yes, go to a bar, if that's what he wants.

Through your willing demeanor and lack of insecurity, you give your husband the message of trust, respect, support, encouragement, patience, privacy, freedom, choice, it's okay to have fun, and the ultimate coveted anticipation of his return. He will appreciate your softer feminine side and crave it after hanging out with "the boys."

When Glenn comes home, he snuggles up next to me and tells me he loves me and that he's thankful he's married. That's the bonus—he appreciates me. His single buddies tell him, privately, that he's lucky to have a wife like me, and he's thankful to have a loving woman waiting for him at home. Be sure to love him up as soon he arrives back home to you. (Very important!)

If you plan on staying married a long time, you'll need to let him go and come back often. Smile as he leaves, tell him to have a great time, and let him know that you'll be waiting for him. Then, savor your time alone! Go have a girls' night out or stay in. I like to take a long, hot, luxurious bubble bath and watch a movie in my pajamas while I indulge in eating a warm Hazelnut Chocolate Panini with Raspberry Dip.

Hazelnut Chocolate Panini and Raspberry Dip (v)

Prep time: 10 minutes
Cook time: 5 minutes
Serves: Makes 2 panini

CHOCOLATE PANINI

4 slices brioche bread (a delicate, but rich and buttery French bread)
1 cup Nutella hazelnut chocolate spread
¼ cup chopped roasted hazelnuts
¼ cup melted butter

RASPBERRY DIP

½ cup raspberry preserves
1 teaspoon fresh squeezed lemon juice
½ teaspoon honey

Spread Nutella on one side of each slice of bread and sprinkle it with the hazelnuts. Fold bread slices together, making a chocolate sandwich, and lightly brush both outside slices with melted butter. Grill on panini grill 5 minutes until golden brown and the chocolate is melting. Whisk together the three ingredients for the raspberry dip.

PRESENTATION

Just because you are eating wicked and warm Hazelnut Chocolate Panini and Raspberry Dip all by yourself, in your pajamas, in front of the TV, does not mean that you shouldn't present it to yourself as if you were serving a guest. Place your panini and dip on a pretty plate, and if you have some fresh raspberries, decorate the plate with them.

Sex
The gift

Husbands connect emotionally through sex. This is how they let their guard down, how they relax, and how they communicate with you and express love. Males are not as vocal as females (no surprise here). But, as explained to me by Glenn, by making love, they express their emotion and love for you. This is how they "tell" you they love you. They show you. It's something that they do with no other person, and it's not just physical.

Give love and sex to your husband often. Be creative, adventurous, and daring. Act out fantasies. Allow yourself the physical enjoyment, the emotional connection, the exhilaration, and the relaxed loving feeling you will share. Don't be afraid to teach your mate how to please you. There are many resources available to help you develop in this regard. If there are unusual issues surrounding sex such as abuse (now or previously), addictive behaviors, lack of desire, or fear of sex, then please seek a professional counselor whom you can trust.

As one of my long-time married girlfriends says, "Don't cut him off!" You'll cut off your marriage, your husband's way to express love, and your life. Some women don't cut him off, but can be controlling about the time, place, and frequency of sex. They control whether their spouse is deserving of some nookie. Women have a lot of power in this regard, and it can be used in a negative way, unfortunately. A woman knows she can use sex to get her man to do anything she wants. Men will do what the woman wants out of thankfulness—first, that he "got some" and, second, in hope that he'll get some more. Withholding sex or using it in a controlling way can create an unhealthy, dysfunctional dynamic. Neither spouse really likes it. It creates resentments.

Men want to be loved, fed, appreciated, laughed with, listened to, and sexed. He married you because he thought that you were the best woman to fulfill him and to please him. Live up to that honor. I believe men are easy to please. Think about what it is like to be your husband and married to *you*. Then, you'll know what to do.

Shortly after writing this chapter, I asked a friend who was hosting a dinner party and who has been married much longer than I have, "What's the secret to your marriage?" Within seconds, she responded unabashed, in front of her guests, "The Gift. I give him sex. The gift of sex."

You've got thirty minutes for an afternoon quickie before the oven timer dings …

Luscious Lemon Squares (v)

They melt in your mouth and leave you aching for more.
A tart, tangy, sweet topping covers a buttery shortbread crust.

Prep time: 10 minutes for the crust; 10 minutes for the topping
Bake time: 15 minutes for the crust; plus 30 more minutes with the topping
Serves: Makes 12 squares

CRUST
2 cups all-purpose, un-sifted flour
½ cup confectioners' sugar
1 cup chilled butter, cut into small pieces (2 cubes of butter)

Preheat your oven to 350°F.
With a pastry cutter (or two dinner knives), cut the flour, sugar, and butter until it resembles fine crumbs. Crumble it with your fingertips at the end and then press the dough firmly into the bottom of a 12- x 8- x 2-inch baking pan. Bake the crust for 15 minutes until the crust is firm. Do not let it brown.

LEMON TOPPING
4 eggs
1¾ cups granulated sugar
2½ tablespoons grated lemon peel and lemon zest
½ cup freshly squeezed lemon juice (about 5 lemons)
½ cup all-purpose flower
½ teaspoon of baking powder

While your crust is baking, make the lemon topping. Whisk the eggs and sugar in a medium-sized bowl. When grating the lemon, use the small holes on your grater and do not include the white part of the lemon; it has a bitter taste. Whisk in remaining ingredients. Pour the lemon mixture over the hot crust and bake 30 minutes until center is firm.

PRESENTATION
Let cool and cut into squares. I like to pile them on a glass cake dish and sift confectioners' sugar over them for a finishing touch.

$\mathcal{M}$anhood

Men are easy to please

$\mathcal{A}$ man's instinctive nature is to hunt, to conquer, to eat, and to rest. This is a man's perfectly simple design. They repeat it daily. They are easy to please. Fulfilling these four simple needs feeds a man's happiness. This is not to say that you are inferior to your man or that you compromise yourself or your strength in anyway while giving your man what he needs. To the contrary. We women know we can do just about anything that men can do in terms of careers, decision making, leadership, sports, money, or anything else we want to pursue. That's why it is so important to let your man be a *man* and let him wear the pants at least half the time.

THE HUNT

$\mathcal{F}$lirt with your man. Be playful and coy. Be witty, sarcastic, hard to get, sassy, saucy, sexy, and a tease. Be feminine! Get him to hunt you, want you, crave you, desire you, and need you.

THE CONQUER

$\mathcal{L}$et him win. Let him be in charge. Let him make decisions. Let him "conquer." (And, for goodness sake, let him open the door and order the wine.) His maleness will rise up attractively, securely, and confidently. He will be proud to be your man, your husband, your leader, and your "hero."

THE FEEDING

The old adage remains true. The way to a man's heart is through his stomach.

THE RESTING

A rested man is a happy man, and I don't just mean sleeping. I mean letting him watch sports all day once in awhile or lay on the couch with a book or lounge an extra hour in bed on Saturday before you hit him with the "honey do" list. He needs to know that home is not another workplace or a battleground. Your home needs to be a restful haven where he comes to replenish his strength and should be the most important place on earth to him.

Chilled Garlic Lime Cilantro Prawn Cocktail

Here's my final sexy and savory tip.
After you've let him "hunt and conquer you," make him a spicy Bloody
Mary and a Chilled Garlic Lime Cilantro Prawn Cocktail. Serve it to
him while he's resting and be sure to make one for you.

Prep time: 30 minutes
Cook time: None
Serves: Makes 2 prawn cocktails

MARINATED PRAWNS
2 cups precooked prawns
A handful of fresh mint, chopped
A handful of fresh cilantro, chopped
The juice of a freshly squeezed lime
The juice of ½ of a freshly squeezed lemon
1 teaspoon grated fresh ginger
1 garlic clove, minced
1 tablespoon olive oil
A pinch of red chili flakes
A pinch of sugar
Sea salt
Freshly ground pepper

In a large bowl toss together all the ingredients and let the prawns
marinate in the refrigerator for no longer than 1 hour, while you make
a complementary aïoli.

PRAWN COCTAIL AÏOLI:
A handful of fresh cilantro, chopped
1 garlic clove, crushed
The juice of a freshly squeezed lime
The juice ½ of a freshly squeezed lemon
A pinch of red chili flakes

1 cup mayonnaise
Sea salt
Fresh ground pepper

Combine the ingredients for the aïoli in a mixing bowl and puree with
your magic wand.

PRESENTATION

In a chilled martini cocktail glass place a small amount of lettuce greens
(spring mix out of the bag) and a very large dollop aïoli on top of the
greens. Hang the marinated prawns around the rim of the glass with
the tails out and add another large dollop of aïoli in the center.

Walk toward your future, together.

*Y*our Chapter

*Th*is chapter is for you, dear reader. It follows the lessons in the book and is intended for you to reflect and to write more tips, notes, recipes, reminders, and inspirations to deepen the intimacy of your marriage. It can be a useful tool to refer back to throughout your marriage. Add to it and change it as your marriage grows, while you choose to be happily wed.

Flirt

Today I will flirt with my husband.

This is how I will make him feel good:

_____

_____

_____

_____

_____

_____

_____

My "look of love" beamed toward my man says it all:

_____

_____

_____

_____

These are the ways I can surprise and delight him:

_____
_____
_____
_____
_____
_____
_____
_____

I'm going to spice up our marriage and change our routine by:

_____
_____
_____
_____
_____
_____
_____

What is my "wow" factor?

_____
_____
_____
_____
_____
_____
_____
_____

These are dates I look forward to going on:

_____
_____
_____
_____
_____
_____
_____
_____
_____

Communicate

Today I will work on communicating.

My voice intonation, word choices, and listening skills are improving. I am working on:

_____
_____
_____
_____
_____
_____
_____
_____

These are my positive thoughts and ways I inwardly talk to myself about my husband:

_____
_____
_____
_____
_____
_____
_____
_____

How I can communicate "the right way":

_____
_____
_____
_____
_____
_____
_____
_____

I appreciate my current marriage role and can envision changing it in the future by:

_____
_____
_____
_____
_____
_____
_____
_____

This is how I maintain my marriage:

_____
_____
_____
_____
_____
_____
_____

My husband wants to please me, and here are ways that I can teach him how:

_____
_____
_____
_____

_____
_____
_____
_____

Endure

I have an enduring marriage.

I take care of my emotional and physical health through:

_____
_____
_____
_____
_____
_____
_____
_____

Our married friends and family encourage us. We will spend more time with:

_____
_____
_____
_____
_____
_____
_____
_____

I acknowledge the progress of our unfolding love story:

_____
_____
_____
_____
_____

_____

_____

_____

_____

We have many blessings, and I am thankful for:

_____

_____

_____

_____

_____

_____

_____

_____

_____

We can survive tough times and realign ourselves by:

_____

_____

_____

_____

_____

_____

_____

_____

Love

Today I will show my husband that I love him.

Here are many ways I show my husband respect:

_____

_____

_____

_____

_____

_____
_____
_____
_____

I am grateful to be married to my husband, and I appreciate:

_____
_____
_____
_____
_____
_____
_____
_____

These are the loving ways I honor his family:

_____
_____
_____
_____
_____
_____
_____
_____

I actively, purposefully, and routinely make time for our marriage by:

_____
_____
_____
_____
_____
_____
_____
_____

These are the rituals that bind our marriage together:

_____

_____

_____

_____

_____

_____

_____

_____

_____

Here are ways we can enjoy more fun and laughter in our marriage:

_____

_____

_____

_____

_____

_____

_____

_____

Give

I give freely, openly, and lovingly to my husband.

I support my husband's passions and opportunities to grow, encouraging him to:

_____

_____

_____

_____

_____

_____

_____

_____

Here are the ways I can give my husband his own space:

_____
_____
_____
_____
_____
_____
_____
_____

My husband enjoys these activities without me, and I encourage him to do them:

_____
_____
_____
_____
_____
_____
_____

These are the ways I create more physical intimacy in our relationship:

_____
_____
_____
_____
_____
_____

This is how I let my man be a man:

_____
_____
_____
_____

*E*pilogue

I first fell in love with Glenn's laugh. It resonates light heartedness and contentment. At a crowded party, while we were dating, I heard him laugh from across the room. He laughed deeply and much longer than I expected, and I had to stop my conversation and listen. I remember thinking, *I could listen to that laugh for the rest of my life.* Even now, his laugh captures my attention when I hear it from a distance. It makes me happy, hearing his pleasure. I still think I could listen to his laugh the rest of my life. It is the sound of his soul.

I love this man, my husband; he is my best friend. We share an appetite for life that is robust. We anticipate a good life together and tell each other this. We anticipate fun, success, and a deepening love. We have youthful attitudes toward life. We share a philosophy of positive expectation, keep an element of surprise alive, and have desire for adventure, which keeps us vibrant. We fantasize about and visualize our lives, and then we pursue our dreams. We love to tantalize each other with a phrase that leads to interesting conversations. One of us will say, "How about this idea …?" adding a long pause and a smile, while the other curiously awaits the unexpected.

When people learn that we've been married over twenty years, we are often asked, "What is the secret recipe?" Well, there are many. Handfuls of them work simultaneously at different intervals. The ones I share with you are just a glimpse of the dynamics between a husband and wife on the journey of a good marriage. As you celebrate your anniversaries, I implore you to inspire other married couples with your stories.

If I had to narrow down all of my recipes to just one, it would be choice. Choose marriage, choose commitment, choose half full, and choose to flirt, to communicate, to love, to endure, and to give. Choose a happy life and choose to be a happy wife.

Delenee

About the Author

Delenee Brugman has cooked more than 15,000 meals for her husband during twenty-one years of marriage. She is a charming host, epicurean, and cook of simple culinary delights. With her husband, Glenn, she co-created a popular Portland café. Both her recipes of food and recipes of love have been lovingly honed with the passage of time.

Endeavors supporting women, children, animals, education, and the preservation of the environment are Delenee's personal and professional passions. She holds a Bachelor of Science Degree in Business Economics from the University of California, Santa Barbara.

She is currently co-authoring *A Happy Wife = A Happy Life*, written with her husband, Glenn.

LaVergne, TN USA
11 October 2009
160459LV00004B/5/P